Quilting
by Hand

Quilting by Hand

HAND-CRAFTED, MODERN
QUILTS AND ACCESSORIES
FOR YOU AND YOUR HOME

Riane Elise

Photography by Rebecca Stumpf

Hardie Grant

QUADRILLE

Publishing Director Sarah Lavelle
Senior Commissioning Editor Harriet Butt
Project Editor Zia Mattocks
Technical Editor Yvonne Fuchs
Head of Design Claire Rochford
Senior Designer Gemma Hayden
Photographer Rebecca Stumpf
Photographer's Assistant Drew Bennett
Stylist Molly O'Connell
Models Reanne Chase, Molly O'Connell,
   Matthew Menardi, Ellie Menardi
Illustrator Riane Elise
Locations Macy Evonosky of @wanderingmyhome,
   Laura Siekman of Mtn Town Design
Head of Production Stephen Lang
Production Controller Katie Jarvis

English language edition published in 2021 by Quadrille,
an imprint of Hardie Grant Publishing

Quadrille
52–54 Southwark Street
London SE1 1UN
quadrille.com

Cataloguing in Publication Data: a catalogue record for this book
is available from the British Library.

ISBN 978 1 78713 612 0
Printed in China

CONTENTS

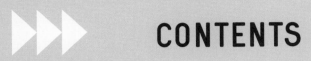

INTRODUCTION

Quilts have always been part of my life, ever since I can remember. My favourite childhood blanket was a soft, pink-and-white quilt made by my mother before I was born. I can still remember burying my face in the fabric and being comforted by the smell, which represented love, contentment and family, all rolled into one. I used that quilt until it fell apart; I remember running back into the house to retrieve it before a drive in the car, and being tucked into bed with it at night. A quilt is almost like a friend, especially during childhood. It can be a constant companion and, for me, a reminder of the love of my family.

Over the years, I have snuggled under so many quilts. On trips to Grandma's house, quilts were the bedding of choice, and always with the knowledge that they had been handmade with love. As I grew up, though, I didn't think much about quilts. I loved to craft with my mother, sister, grandmothers and aunts, but for some reason I resisted sewing. I was surrounded by creative women, who always seemed to have a box, a cupboard or an entire a room full of

supplies that we would transform into beautiful and functional objects, and the quilts were always there in the background.

Towards the end of my college education, I had the opportunity to work at a magazine that focused on design, handcraft and curating well-made, beautiful things for the home. It opened my eyes to the world of modern design and making, and I relished learning about new ideas, techniques and objects that could be made by hand. At the same time, I also turned my gaze towards sewing. As a young adult with little spending money, I wanted to learn how to make garments, or alter charity-shop finds into chic, custom clothing. I asked my grandmother to teach me to sew, but rather than starting with garments (a difficult undertaking, to be sure), she bought me a quilt pattern and gave me unfettered access to her fabric bins.

Over the course of a summer, we made that first quilt together. She taught me how to sew a block, how to stitch the blocks together, how to baste the layers of the quilt and, finally, how

to quilt it by hand. Every step provided a new challenge, but hand quilting was by far the most difficult. I couldn't make my hands hold the tiny needle and "rock" it the way my grandma could. My stitches were uneven and my fingers hurt, but she told me, "You'll love this quilt so much better if you hand-quilt it." I didn't understand what she meant at the time, as I struggled to finish a line on the queen-sized quilt. But the more I practised, the more I began to see.

A few years after I learned to quilt from my grandmother, my friend Deb introduced me to "big stitch" hand quilting. Once I tried stitching with the larger needle and thread, I was hooked, and began finishing all my quilts by hand, developing my own unique style. From that point on, handwork became the pillar of my creative life, a daily practice.

Of course, before the invention of the sewing machine in the mid-nineteenth century, all quilts were made by hand, and for centuries, "hand quilting" was simply "quilting". Over the years, quilts have been finished with all types of handwork – small stitching, large stitching, intricate and precise motifs and loose hand tying, even with stunning embroidery. Machine quilting, while ubiquitous now, is a fairly new approach to quilting when you consider the long practice of handwork. As I journeyed further into my sewing practice, I had a deep desire to create quilts entirely by hand, and I picked up the art of hand piecing (sewing each patchwork seam by hand). Like hand quilting, hand piecing was, for centuries, the way early quilters sewed

their tops. It takes time and patience, but a hand-pieced quilt is as unique as a fingerprint, and the small variations and organic seams show the hand of the maker. I still love inspecting old quilts, carefully pulling back the fabric to see the maker's careful stitches and how they hold fast, even decades later.

Handwork has a special way of connecting us, to our heritage, to modern handicraft and to ourselves. Each time I quilt, I'm reminded of that tradition, which is not limited by era, birthplace, race, creed or social status. We are linked by the stitches, whether made for pleasure or by necessity, and it is a special thing to be connected to this tradition and to each other by something as simple as fabric, fibres, needle and thread.

For me, handwork in its various forms is meditative and centring. It is often the anchor that grounds me when things seem to be shifting under my feet and has helped me work through problems and anxieties, keeping my hands busy and my mind free to wander. I love spending a Sunday morning with a quilt in hand, sipping coffee and dialling up a friend for a long chat.

As you begin your hand-quilting journey (or tread ever further along the path), I hope the magic of hand quilting takes hold and you discover ways to make this tradition your own. In this book, I aim to teach you the joy of hand quilting, just as the women in my life have done for me – through thoughtful instructions and an appreciation for the simple joy of making – but how you use the contents within these pages is up to you.

I can't wait to see what you make, and I hope you enjoy the journey.

Happy stitching,

"THE HAND-QUILTING TRADITION IS ALIVE AND WELL TODAY. IT'S NOT FANCY. YOU DON'T NEED ANYTHING SPECIAL — JUST A FEW SIMPLE TOOLS AND A WILLINGNESS TO WORK THROUGH EACH STITCH BY HAND."

HOW TO USE THIS BOOK

This book will serve as your guide to making quilts by hand – with as much or as little handwork as you'd like to take on. Each pattern has instructions for piecing the quilt, which can be done by hand or by machine. All the examples featured in the book have been quilted by hand with a mix of techniques, and instructions are provided if you'd like to re-create the quilting in the samples.

The basic techniques for hand piecing and quilting are contained on pages 28–51, and other helpful tips are scattered throughout the book and within the patterns.

Many of the quilt patterns include templates for more easily piecing shapes like triangles and curves. You can find and download the templates at riane-elise.com/quilting-by-hand. For more about using templates, you can reference the "Cutting and using templates" section on page 28.

This book has been written to be as friendly as possible for quilters using either the metric or imperial systems of measurement. As most quilt patterns and rulers use the imperial system, and the standard quilting seam allowance is ¼in, the quilts in this book have been designed imperial first, with friendly tips and conversions for metric. To gain a better understanding of the measurements and conversions used in this book, refer to the "Measurements" section on page 23.

And if you come across a term you aren't familiar with, don't worry! There is a handy glossary on page 190 that can be your quick reference to all things quilting.

As you embark on this hand-quilting journey, I encourage you to explore new hand-quilting motifs or to put your unique touch on the ideas and techniques presented in this book. The beauty of quilts, after all, is that they are unique to the maker, and I like to think of a handmade quilt as being as specific to someone as their fingerprint. As you explore your own style, I hope you find approaches that bring a distinctiveness and joy to your practice.

INSPIRATION

I believe in finding inspiration as much in the ordinary as in the exciting. The quilts in this book embody that dichotomy of embracing the whirlwinds of change and adventure, and also settling intentionally into the everyday. The making of this book spanned nearly a year, and during that time, I experienced both sides of this coin very deeply. Early in the process, I was able to travel extensively for work and pleasure. My sister and I went on our first solo trip together, exploring some of Europe's great cities. I travelled the USA for work and was on the road for weeks on end. I am grateful for every new experience, every moment of wonder, and especially how travel encourages me to crave the routine of being at home.

Then of course, everything changed in the spring of 2020, and I, along with the rest of the world, went through a period of deep settling in. My husband and I bought a house and shifted our attention to making it into a home, thoughtfully transforming it with new paint, small projects and big dreams for what it would someday become. I learned how to cultivate fulfilment within the four walls of our home, and adapted to navigating the world more carefully and with more intention.

The quilts in this book are a direct reflection of all that has transpired during those seasons. Some of the designs embody the excitement of travel and change. Others focus on simplicity and quiet beauty. And, of course, the handwork is both my creative outlet and emotional salve when the sands begin to shift.

For my process, I generally create a collection of quilt designs all at once, based on the themes – both visual and emotional – that are coursing through my life at the time. I turn my computer on, throw on some headphones and some good music, and sketch shapes and motifs that inspire me. Often, by the time I'm done with a round of sketches, I have several quilts that I can't wait to make, and sometimes get sidetracked by quickly testing a block or concept.

What I like best about this process is that each collection is like a time capsule. Certain quilts may look abstract, but they often represent something special or are linked to the memory of a happy time. For example, Porta (page 118) was inspired by the architecture in Lisbon, seen on that trip to Europe with my sister. It was a joy to look through my photos as I sought inspiration for this quilt. Pines (page 76) was sparked by the Rocky Mountains in Colorado and a celebration of our new home. The curves in Parlour (page 84) remind me of the windows, doors and arches in a home, but I hand pieced this quilt on a road trip through Nevada. Ritual (page 168) is a modern interpretation of a very old, traditional quilt block that has been made for centuries under different names. I couldn't wait to embrace that history and tradition, so it was the first quilt I made for this book. Steady (page 70) reminds me of the beauty and joy of simple, easy sewing, and was the first quilt I made in our new home, when I needed a fun, reliable project to jumpstart my creativity after the move.

Each quilt fully embodies the polarities of adventure and grounding, excitement and settling, but their designs take on even more meaning as the making process continues to inform their stories. As you make these quilts, I encourage you to remember the thoughts, feelings and events that are dominating your life at the time, and see if those memories come back to you as you enjoy the quilts in the years to come. They are now as much a part of your story as they are mine, and they will take on their own meanings as you create and use them in your own unique way.

DESIGNING YOUR OWN QUILTS

If you're like me, sometimes a pattern serves as a great starting point and introduces a certain technique, but once you get the hang of it, you may want to alter the design to better suit your needs or aesthetic – or you may even be inspired to design your own quilts. I've been there myself, and this sense of curiosity led me over time to developing my own style.

Most quilt patterns are built using the same common elements – triangles, squares, rectangles, circle components, borders, etc. It's the combination of these shapes that makes a unique quilt pattern, and once you know how to make the building blocks, you can combine them in myriad ways to make a design that speaks to you.

To familiarize yourself with some of the basics, I recommend referencing the simple patchwork in the Curio quilt (page 142), or the flying geese in Pines (page 76). Ritual's half-square triangles (page 168) are some of the most common units of quiltmaking, and the quarter-circles in Centro or Sylvan (pages 110 and 154) are a great foundation for quilting with curves. Once you learn how to make these shapes, you can begin mixing and matching them into your own unique designs.

I recommend sketching your ideas before you begin to determine the size, scale and placement of your blocks. Graph paper is a great place to start, or you can use a computer program like Adobe Illustrator, which is my preferred design method.

You can also use the tips in the "Scaling Patterns" section of this book (page 24) to alter individual blocks to a size that fits your needs. Borders and rectangles can be added to increase the size of your quilt or incorporate negative space (more background space around the focal point of your quilt). Early in my quilt design days, I would cut large pieces of fabric, sew them to my quilt top and trim to fit. This improvisational method is great for beginning quilt designers as you don't need to pre-determine sizing (or do much maths). Sometimes the easiest way to start is simply sewing pieces of fabric together.

FINDING YOUR VOICE

As you're designing, pay attention to the shapes, colours, textures and quilting styles that most inspire you. Over time, you may see trends emerge – perhaps they echo the styles you incorporate into your wardrobe, home design or other hobbies. Pay attention to that aesthetic, and make a lot of quilts (even if they're small pieces) to cultivate your creative voice. You may find that your style emerges quickly, or it could take years of experimenting. For my part, I designed dozens of quilts over the course of several years before I developed my own unique style. Once I recognized it, I designed a collection of 15 quilts that were the first true patterns in my voice. They were published in my first book, *Inheritance,* and since then, I've continued to grow and evolve, incorporating new shapes and colours into my aesthetic, but have always remained true to that original voice. Your journey may be different, but with practice and a willingness to explore, your aesthetic will emerge and produce a creative voice that is uniquely yours.

MATERIALS

There are many amazing quilting tools and materials – and, as any quilter will attest, sometimes the hardest part of quilting is choosing your fabrics. During the nearly ten years I've been quilting, I've tried my hand at many different materials and slowly discovered what works best for me. I've outlined some of my favourites here, but I encourage you to try both the materials that are readily available to you and some new ones. Experimentation is the best way to find what you like and, if you're like me, once you find your groove, you'll never look back.

FABRIC

Many quilters start off with quilting cotton as their fabric of choice, as it keeps its shape when cutting and piecing, which makes for clean, accurate quilts. Quilting cotton is also affordable, comes in many colours and patterns, and is readily available from most quilting or fabric shops around the world.

That said, I love using a linen/cotton blend for my quilts, and most of the quilts in this book are made with fabric composed of 55 per cent linen and 45 per cent cotton. I also love other linen blends with a bit of stretch, so I've also used a knit fabric made from 55 per cent linen and 45 per cent rayon. This rayon blend makes a beautiful, drapey backing and produces a soft and snuggly quilt that has a lot of texture. It's also fun to hand quilt with, so maybe consider trying a knit blend such as this for one of your hand-quilting projects.

Choosing fabric is one of the most enjoyable aspects of quilting, so go for a browse at your local fabric or craft shop and choose what inspires you.

See also pages 23 and 36 for information on fabric widths.

BATTING OR WADDING

Batting, or wadding, is the layer of fibre inside the quilt, and the material you choose will have significant impact on the finished quilt. Cotton and cotton blends are some of the most common batting choices for quilters. They are lightweight and versatile, and come in various "lofts" (plushness), so you can pick the texture you want.

All of the quilts in this book use wool batting, which I like for its high loft and strong but malleable fibres. Wool is lovely for hand quilting, and produces a textured quilt that is warm and comfortable.

For lighter-weight quilts, I recommend bamboo batting. There are also sustainable polyester battings, made from recycled water bottles, which quilt up beautifully.

THREAD

Some quilters have a large stash of fabric – I have a large stash of thread. I absolutely love thread and, as a hand quilter, it seems like one of the most personal materials in the quilt-making process. I love experimenting, but I also love coming back to a tried-and-true thread that I know will provide hours of joy.

HAND-QUILTING THREAD

I like to call my style of quilting "high-contrast hand quilting". The stitching stands on its own as a design element due to the thick thread and large stitches, which are more visible than those made with traditional hand-quilting thread, which is much thinner and produces smaller stitches.

In my work, I use mostly sashiko thread, which is a multi-ply cotton thread with Japanese origins. Sashiko thread has been used for generations to decorate garments and home goods, as well as to strengthen textiles. It comes in skeins, much like yarn, and pairs well with a special sashiko needle, which has a sharp tip and a larger eye to accommodate the thread's thickness.

You can also use a thick thread, such as perle cotton, embroidery floss or 12-weight thread, to achieve high contrast in your quilting. Again, I encourage you to experiment with different thread types to find out what works best for your quilting style.

HAND-PIECING THREAD

The thread used for hand piecing is an undersung hero of the thread world. Because we place each stitch by hand, it's important that the thread is strong enough to hold the seam, but light enough to blend into the quilt and let the piecing and quilting shine.

For the strongest seams, I recommend glazed or glace cotton, which has been treated and coated with wax or resin to strengthen the fibres. I like it for hand piecing because it rarely tangles, and it holds up to tugs and snags. I also like to use a strong thread, such as 50-weight cotton, which is slightly thinner than glazed cotton but also quite strong.

MACHINE-PIECING THREAD

The best machine thread is one that you rarely have to think about. It doesn't break or cause lint build-up in your machine, and comes in many colours that you can match to your fabrics. I recommend a medium- to lightweight (about 40 weight to 80 weight) cotton or cotton blend. As before, experiment with a few different brands and weights to find the thread that works best for you and your machine.

NEEDLES

Needles come in all shapes and sizes, but my rule of thumb when it comes to choosing the right needle is to use what feels best to you. I didn't like the traditional hand-quilting needles my grandmother gave me when we were making our first quilt (and honestly, I still don't).

For hand piecing and binding, I prefer to use bigger needles than most quilters, often reaching for a size 3 or 4 sharp, rather than an 8, 9 or 10.

For hand quilting, I almost exclusively use sashiko needles, which I like because they are perfectly suited for my favourite sashiko thread, and they are often very long and very sharp. Sashiko needles come in different lengths, so try a few and see which you like best. Often, I choose long needles for making long, straight lines, and shorter needles for sewing curves. You can also use large-eye embroidery needles for hand quilting, if those are more readily available.

CUTTING TOOLS

Most quilters use a rotary cutter, cutting mat and quilting ruler to cut their pieces, and I recommend that you pick up these essentials if you don't already have them. For straight lines, a rotary cutter gives a nice, accurate cut; it's also extremely helpful when making quilts comprising small pieces or many pieces (such as Curio, page 142). I like a 45mm rotary cutter and a big, self-healing cutting mat of at least 24 x 36in (61 x 91cm), though a smaller one will do.

You may also want a good pair of fabric shears, especially for cutting out curves and other pieces made from templates. I like my 8in (20cm) dressmaker shears, which are sharp and heavy.

NOTIONS

There are so many tools that can make sewing easier and more enjoyable, but I believe that the simplest route is often the best, so I won't encourage you to buy or use anything other than the necessities. I started quilting without a thimble, but now I can't sew without my trusty leather thimble. I don't use a hoop or frame for hand quilting, but you may find that you prefer one. You may want a needle threader, to ease the burden on your eyes and fingers. For marking, I like a standard mechanical pencil or a mechanical chalk pencil, but you may prefer an erasable-ink marker or a hera marker. Half the fun of quilting is discovering which tools bring you joy in the process, so please put them to the test and see what works best for you.

SEWING MACHINE

While this book focuses primarily on the art and craft of quilting by hand, it can be helpful to have a sewing machine on hand for piecing, binding or various other sewing needs. I use vintage sewing machines inherited from my grandma and my husband's grandmother. Vintage machines are often workhorses, and even though there are some incredibly sophisticated sewing machines on the market, I like the heft and reliability of my older machines and the stories that come with them.

If you don't yet own a sewing machine, you can certainly buy one from a local sewing shop, or you may want to scour flea markets and secondhand shops for a vintage machine. Whatever machine you have, I suggest purchasing a ¼in foot (also called a patchwork foot) and a walking foot as your default components. You don't need much beyond these elements to make any quilt in this book – and, of course, every quilt can be made entirely by hand.

MEASUREMENTS

While I recognize that the majority of the global population uses the metric system, quilting measurements are often based on the imperial system. Seam allowances, cutting quantities, block measurements and quilt sizing are generally measured in inches, and the "quarter inch" seam allowance is the ubiquitous standard used for patchwork.

The patterns in this book are written using the imperial system as their foundation, but if that is not your native measurement system, fear not. I've included metric conversions for fabric requirements, finished quilt sizes, seam allowances and other helpful measurements.

For metric users, I recommend picking up a few helpful items as you begin your quilting journey. An imperial quilting ruler (also called a patchwork ruler) will be your best friend when cutting fabric and trimming blocks and finished quilts. I recommend choosing one of at least 6 x 24in from a trusted brand. I also recommend purchasing a patchwork foot for your sewing machine, which will provide a ¼in seam allowance with no measuring required.

Armed with these tools and the helpful guide below, you only need to follow the pattern instructions using imperial measurements to produce quilts of the proper size and scale.

WIDTH OF FABRIC

Throughout this book, "width of fabric" is abbreviated to "WOF" and simply refers to the width of fabric when it is unfolded from the bolt. A standard-width of fabric is about 42–45in (107–114cm), while some wide fabrics come in widths from 54–56 (137–142cm).

The patterns in this book are written for both widths, and you can refer to the information in each pattern for how to approach the cutting and sewing instructions based on the fabric you are using. Less fabric will be needed when using larger widths of fabric, so read through the fabric requirements before purchasing any new fabric or beginning a project.

SCALING PATTERNS

Many of the patterns in this book can be scaled to smaller or larger sizes. In most cases, you can multiply the width and length of the finished fabric pieces by 150 per cent or 200 per cent to make a larger version, or multiply them by 75 per cent or 50 per cent to make a smaller version. The key here is that the finished size must be multiplied appropriately, and then the seam allowance must be added back in.

For example, if a pattern calls for squares cut to 6½ x 6½in, the finished size is 6 x 6in, so to make a larger size, you can scale the finished block size up by 150 per cent to get a finished block of 9 x 9in. You would then add the seam allowance back in by adding ½in to reach a cut size of 9½ x 9½in (150 per cent). For the same block, you could scale up by 200 per cent to make your final block 12 x 12in and cut your squares 12½ x 12½in. The same quilt can be scaled down by cutting squares to 5 x 5in (75 per cent) or 3½ x 3½in (50 per cent).

As a rule of thumb, on the facing page are some basic scaling conversions for quilt sizes.

A WORD OF CAUTION: This method does not work for quilts that require a curved template. However, appropriately sized curved templates can be downloaded at: riane-elise.com/quilting-by-hand

Armed with this knowledge (and a calculator), you can modify any quilt to suit your needs.

	Scale for Baby	Scale for Throw	Scale for Twin
Baby 30 x 40in	–	200 per cent	250 per cent
Throw 60 x 70in	50 per cent	–	125 per cent
Twin 70 x 90in	50 per cent	75 per cent	–
Queen 92 x 104in	50 per cent	66–75 per cent*	75 per cent
King 110 x 108in	33–50 per cent*	50–66 per cent*	75 per cent

	Scale for Queen	Scale for King
Baby 30 x 40in	300 per cent	350 per cent
Throw 60 x 70in	150 per cent	175 per cent
Twin 70 x 90in	125 per cent	150 per cent
Queen 92 x 104in	–	–
King 110 x 108in	–	–

*You can also scale by thirds, but this works best with quilts that have a finished size and pieces divisible by three. If your quilt is not divisible by three, I recommend scaling up to the next closest 25 per cent.

▶▶▶ THE TECHNIQUES ▶▶▶▶▶

THE TECHNIQUES

These techniques are the building blocks of quilting, and with a little practice, you'll be able to not only make the quilts in this book, but any quilt you choose. If any of these techniques are new to you, a small word of advice: practise, let go of perfection, modify to suit your own style and, of course, enjoy the process. Whatever feels good to you is the "right" way.

CUTTING AND USING TEMPLATES

Some of the quilts in this book require the use of templates to cut out patchwork pieces. Refer to the pattern for the correct scale at which to print or copy the template.

Downloadable PDF templates are also available at riane-elise.com/quilting-by-hand. All templates include seam allowances – simply trace the template onto your fabric as indicated, and cut out the shape using fabric shears. The patchwork pieces are then ready for assembling.

PIECING

Sewing patchwork pieces together to construct the quilt top is referred to as "piecing". The quilts in this book are designed to be constructed either by hand or machine. To fully embrace handwork, you may choose to sew each patchwork piece by hand and then hand-quilt to finish, resulting in an entirely handmade quilt. Whatever the amount of handwork you choose, use this piecing guide to aid you on your journey.

PIECING BY HAND

For hand piecing, the only tools required are a needle, thread, marking tool (I prefer a pencil) and fabric. A thimble can also be helpful if you like to use one (I love my trusty leather thimble).

1. Begin by marking the seam line on the wrong side of one of the patchwork pieces you'll be sewing. Mark ¼in (6mm) away from the raw edge in a line. Cut a length of strong thread (I favour traditional hand-quilting thread, or glazed cotton, at least a 50 weight). Tie a knot in one end and thread the other through a thin needle (I like sharps in sizes 3–9, and I usually use a size 4).

2. Place the fabric pieces right sides together and insert your needle at one end on the marked line. Stitch along the marked line using small stitches – about ⅛in (3mm) long. I recommend backstitching after every four to five stitches, which will help secure the seam.

3. Sew across the length of the seam and tie off with several stitches in the same spot or a sturdy knot. Trim the thread.

4. I press my hand-sewn seams open, but you may press them to one side if you prefer.

As you hand-piece the quilt top, you may need to mark additional lines over the seams. I often mark my seam lines as I sew, which is helpful if any prior seams need to be trimmed or if one of my seams isn't a true ¼in (6mm). Marking as I go can produce a more accurate quilt in the end, and if you choose to do this, simply mark ¼in (6mm) from each edge on the wrong side in the same way as above before sewing your next seam.

I particularly like to hand-piece my curves, and some of my favourite quilts to hand-piece in this book are the following: Monta, page 64; Pines, page 76 Parlour, page 84; Lune, page 128; Panto, page 136; and Sylvan, page 154.

PIECING BY MACHINE

If you'd like to complete a quilt top more quickly, machine quilting is a good option. You can always hand-quilt a top, even if you piece it by machine. Many of the quilts in this book were sewn together by machine and finished with hand quilting.

To piece with a machine, I recommend using a ¼in or "patchwork" foot. This type of foot has a guide to achieve the perfect seam allowance for quilting.

You do not need to mark your seam for machine piecing. Simply line up the two fabric pieces, right sides together, and pin in place if desired. Feed the patchwork pieces through your machine using the guide on the ¼in or patchwork foot to create a ¼in (6mm) seam. I recommend a stitch length of about 2–2.5mm. I prefer to press my machine-pieced seams open, but you may press them to the side if you prefer.

Some of my favourite quilts for machine piecing are the following: Steady, page 70; Reflect, page 92; Porta, page 118; Curio, page 142; Union, page 148; Likeness, page 162; and Ritual, page 168.

TIP
You may also want to have a walking foot on hand for piecing together long seams or rows with bulky seams. A walking foot will pull fabric through the machine evenly on the top and bottom layers, making the pieces less likely to shift as you sew. A walking foot is also useful for piecing quilts with bias edges like Monta (page 64) or Pines (page 76).

SEWING CURVES

It isn't as difficult to sew curves as it may seem – especially if you are sewing by hand. Each pattern that uses curves includes a curved template, instructions about what size pieces to cut and whether any prep is needed (some fabric pieces should be folded and pressed prior to cutting). Follow all prep instructions according to the pattern before sewing them together and refer to the images on the following pages to prepare your curved pieces.

See the step images on page 34–35.

1. To prepare to sew curves, mark the seam line along the curved edges of the concave pieces. You can approximate a ¼in (6mm) seam allowance or use the curved template to trace a curve ¼in away from the edge (see step 3). I also suggest marking the midway points on each convex and concave piece for easy alignment.

   Next, snip small notches, about ⅛in (3mm) deep, in the concave pieces inside the marked line. Leave about 1in (2.5cm) between each notch.

2. Align the centre of one concave piece with the centre of one convex piece, right sides together, as shown on page 34 (see step 4). Place the concave piece on top with the marked line facing up. Pin at the centre to hold the pieces in place.

3. Next, pin the right-hand "leg" of the concave piece to the right corner of the convex piece, with the marked line still facing up. Pin the left-hand "leg" of the concave piece to the left corner of the convex piece (as shown on page 34). Place a few more pins along the edges to secure the curved pieces together.

4. Sew the concave piece to the convex piece, following the instructions for hand piecing or machine piecing on pages 30–32. Press the seams as indicated in the pattern to finish.

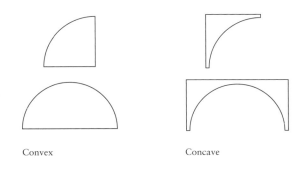

Convex   Concave

TIP
Once you've practised machine piecing a few times, you may not need to mark the seam line. If you are hand-piecing the curved seam, I recommend always marking the ¼in (6mm) seam allowance before sewing.

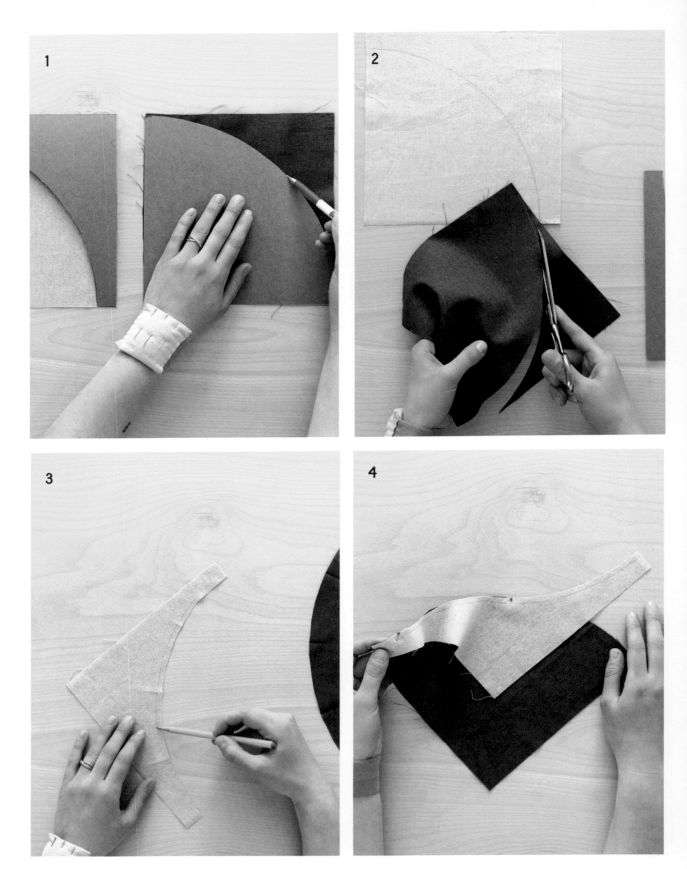

SEWING SEMI-CIRCLES

Sewing a semi-circle is exactly the same as sewing a quarter-circle, but you will trace the template on a folded piece of fabric to create the appropriate shape. Be sure to follow the alignment instructions on the templates when tracing the curves.

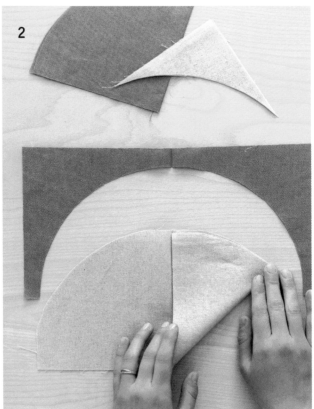

PREPARING
THE BACKING

Quilt backings are generally made up of two or three large pieces of fabric sewn together. A good quilt backing is slightly larger than the quilt top – about 4in (10cm) all round. Each pattern lists the quantity of fabric you'll need to complete the correct-sized backing for your quilt.

To prepare the backing, cut the length of the fabric in half, selvedge to selvedge, to form two fabric rectangles. For example, if the pattern calls for 5yd (4.6m) of backing fabric, you would cut the fabric into two pieces that are 2½yd (2.3m) long each.

Sew the two fabric pieces together along their length, with right sides together. You may want to use a ½in (12mm) seam allowance for extra stability. The seam will run vertically along the back of your quilt, from top to bottom (Diagram 1).

For extra-large quilts, more than 84in (213cm) wide (such as the largest size of Talus, page 100), you may need to use three pieces of fabric if you are using a standard fabric width of 42–44in (107–112cm). To do this, cut the backing yardage length into three equal parts and sew them together lengthways along the trimmed selvage edges. The two seams will run horizontally across the back of the quilt (see Diagram 2).

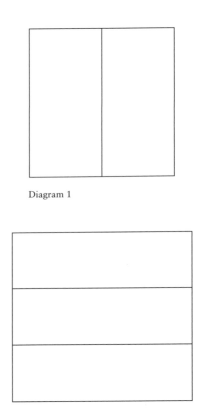

Diagram 1

Diagram 2

MARKING

Two of the most important steps of the hand-quilting process are marking and basting. Good marking will result in clean, crisp quilting lines, and good basting will keep your quilt free of wrinkles and puckers.

I use a mechanical pencil or mechanical chalk pencil for marking, both of which allow me to mark a precise line that can be removed later. You could use an erasable- or washable-ink pen or marker. A hera marker can also be useful, but be careful when you're marking a large quilt, as working the fabric with your hands may cause the marks to disappear before you're finished quilting.

A transparent quilting ruler, at least 24in (61cm) long, is helpful for marking lines and allows you to see the spacing between each line. I found a 72in (183cm) ruler at a local hardware store, and this is very useful for marking long, straight lines on large quilts.

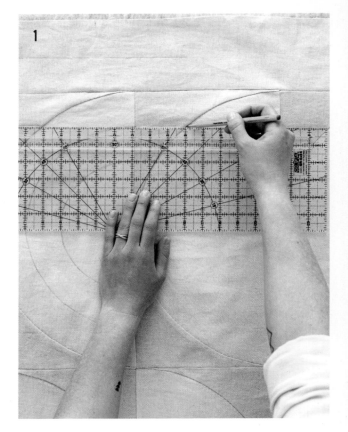

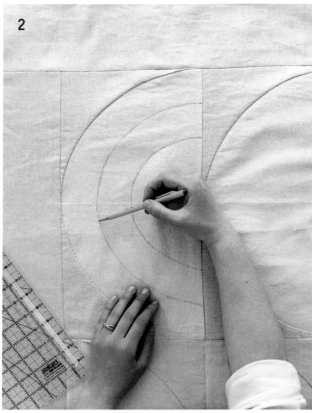

BASTING

Temporarily securing all the quilt's layers together during the quilting process is known as basting. I like to baste using safety pins, but you may choose to use large basting stitches with a contrasting thread. Once the quilting is complete, the basting pins or stitches are removed, and the quilting holds the layers together on its own.

To baste, make your quilt "sandwich" by layering all the elements together. The backing should be on the bottom, with the right side facing down and away from you. (Tape the backing to the floor or a tabletop to smooth out any puckers and wrinkles.) The batting goes next, and the quilt top rests on top of the sandwich, with the right side facing up.

I usually mark my quilting lines at this stage, before basting. Once your quilt sandwich is layered and marked, you can place pins or basting stitches about 3–5in (8–13cm) apart, working your way from the middle outwards. Smooth any wrinkles or puckers as you go, and continue until the quilt is completely basted and ready for quilting.

A NOTE ON BACKING AND BATTING MEASUREMENTS

All backing and batting measurements you'll find in the project pages of this book are approximate. As a rule of thumb, your batting should measure about 2in (5cm) larger than your quilt top, but should just be large enough so your full quilt top can fit comfortably on top. Backing measurements should measure 4-8in (10-20cm) larger than your finished quilt top. After making your quilt sandwich, you can always trim the backing and batting, but cutting larger than you need will ensure you have plenty of room to make your quilt sandwich.

HAND QUILTING

My absolute favourite way to finish a quilt is hand quilting, which has become a form of meditation and art for me. This technique adds a handmade element that is completely unique to the maker and can never be exactly replicated. Furthermore, handwork does not require any special materials, and it's the perfect activity for relaxing in the evening or taking on a trip (I love hand quilting while I'm being driven in a car). Once you start hand quilting, you, like me, may never look back.

Refer to the Materials section on pages 16–21 as you select your hand-quilting tools. I like to use thick sashiko thread, but you may prefer a thinner hand-quilting thread with less contrast.

1. To start quilting, cut a length of thread, tie a knot in one end and thread the other end through your needle. Beginning in the middle of your quilt, pull the needle up through the back of the quilt on one of your marked lines.

2. Hold the backing lightly in one hand and gently pop the knot through to the inner layers to hide it within the quilt sandwich. Make your first stitch by inserting the needle through all the layers, then bring it back up to the top.

3. Your stitches can be any size, but I make mine about ⅛–¼in (3–6mm) in length. As you get more comfortable with quilting, you can load a few stitches onto your needle at a time and work quickly across your marked lines.

4. Continue quilting from the centre outwards, pulling the stitches taut but not too tight as you quilt. Stop quilting about ½in (12mm) from the edge of the quilt, or when you have about 4in (10cm) of thread remaining. Pull your needle and thread through to the back, and make a knot close to the backing fabric. Insert your needle close to the knot into the inner layers and back out to the backing a slight distance away. Gently pull the knot through to the inner layers and trim the thread to finish.

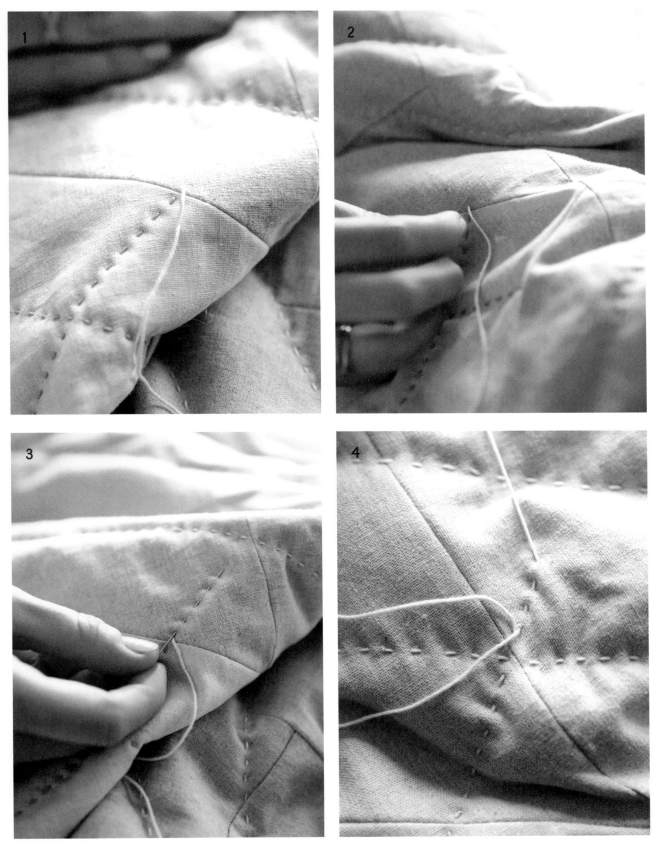

TYING

This means of quilting has been around for centuries, and tying still holds up as a fun and easy way to finish a quilt, especially for beginners. Try these hand-tying techniques on one of your quilts to add texture and personality. For examples of tied quilts, see Curio (page 142), Parlour (page 84) and the Greeting cushions (page 182).

TIP
Depending on your batting (read the guidelines on the packaging), ties can be placed up to 8in (20cm) apart, though I recommend 2–4in (5–10cm).

TRADITIONAL TIES

1. Make a small mark where you'd like to place each tie. Thread your needle, but do not make a knot in either end. Insert your needle through the top of the quilt and thread it through all the layers.

2. Bring it back up to the quilt top about ⅛–¼in (3–6mm) away from where you first inserted it.

3. Trim the thread so the tails are a comfortable length for tying.

4. Tie the tails together using a simple square knot. Repeat to double- or triple-tie the knot. Continue in this fashion throughout the quilt top.

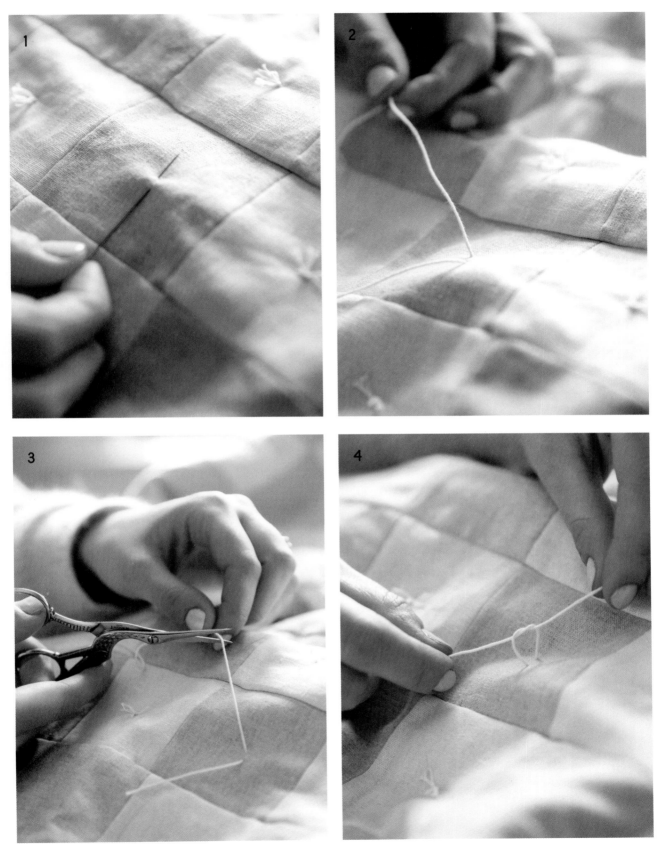

FRENCH-KNOT TIES

1. Make a small mark where you'd like to place each tie. Thread your needle and make a single knot in one end of the thread. Insert the needle through the back of the quilt at one of the marks.

2. Make a French knot by wrapping the thread twice around the needle and inserting the needle back down into the top of the quilt close to the insertion point.

3. Pull the needle all the way through to the back. Trim the tails to a comfortable length for tying and tie them together using a double square knot. Repeat across the quilt top until it is covered with French-knot ties.

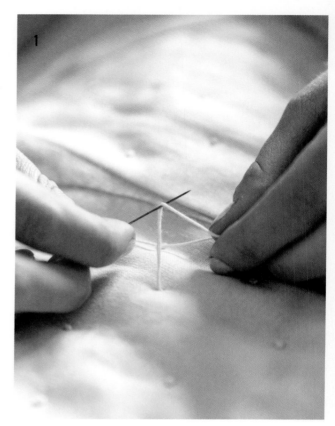

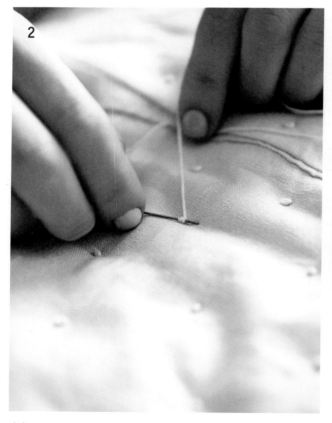

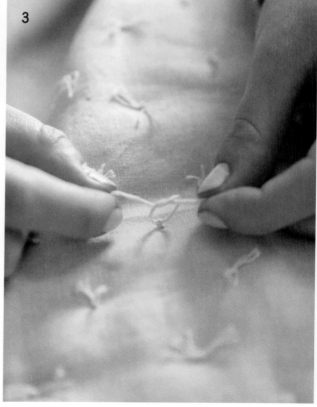

CRISSCROSS TIES

1. Make a small mark where you'd like to place each tie. Thread your needle and make a single knot in one end of the thread. Insert the needle through the back of the quilt, about ¼in (6mm) from one of the marks.

2. Make a diagonal stitch spanning about ½in (12mm) over the mark. Bring the needle back up through the back of the quilt about ¼in (6mm) from your previous entry/exit points, and complete the crisscross stitch by making a second diagonal stitch.

3. Tie off each stitch with a knot. Repeat across the quilt top until complete.

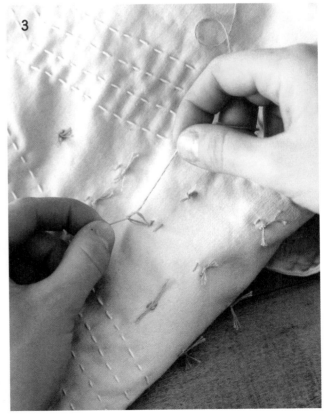

FINISHING YOUR QUILT

After quilting, it's time to finish the quilt by trimming away any excess fabric and adding binding to conceal the raw edges.

Before binding, you'll want to "square up" your quilt, which simply means to trim away the excess fabric and batting, and straighten the edges of your quilt top (see image 1). The best way to do this is to lay the quilt on a table or the floor on top of a cutting mat and use a rotary cutter and quilting ruler to trim a straight edge on each side of your quilt (see images 2 and 3). You can also use the lines on your quilting ruler to ensure the corners are perfect 90-degrees square (see image 4).

To bind, you can follow the instructions on the following pages to attach the binding with a machine or use the backing fabric. Attaching by machine is most common – in this technique, we use a machine to sew a strip of fabric around the perimeter, fold it over the raw edges to cover them and then stitch it in place by hand. However, I also wanted to include the less conventional option to bind without the need for a machine by pulling the backing fabric over to the front and stitching it down by hand. If you use this method, you will be able to make your quilt by hand from start to finish.

TIP
If you're using the backing as the binding, you do not need to cut binding strips as indicated in the patterns.

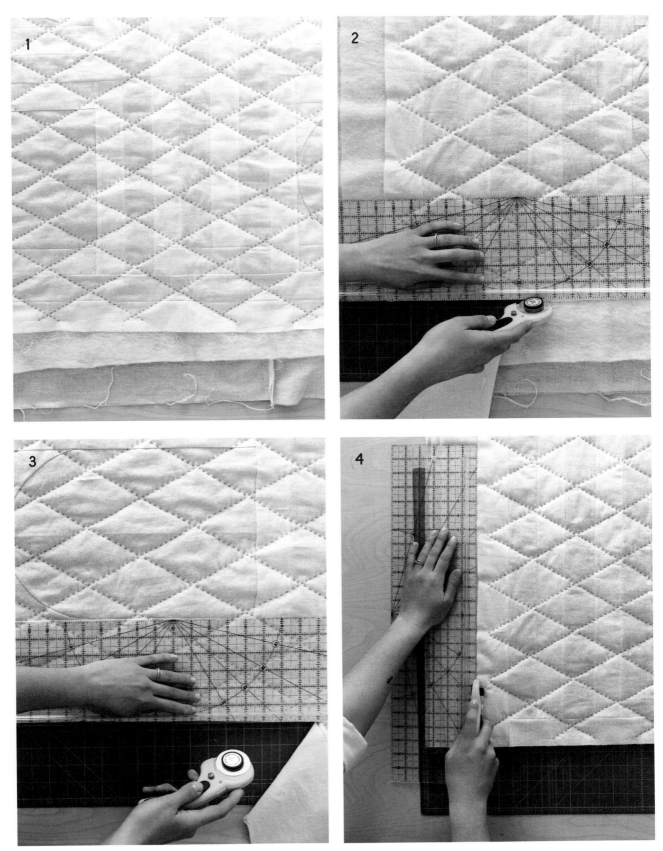

BIND USING THE QUILT BACKING

To bind and finish your quilt completely by hand, you will use your backing fabric to cover the raw edges. After quilting, when you are squaring up the quilt, fold the edges of the backing under the quilt as far as you can so it is out of the way. Trim your quilt top and batting, being careful to avoid cutting the backing (see image 1). Then, trim your backing to exactly 1in (2.5cm) larger than your quilt top and batting all round (see image 2).

Press one side of the backing in half towards your quilt top, then in half again so its width is ¼in (6mm) (see image 3). Repeat for the other three sides. To attach, pull one side of the folded backing to the front of your quilt, and hand-stitch it in place using an invisible or blind stitch (see image 4). Stop about 1–2in (2.5–5cm) from the corner. At the corner, fold the corner of the backing in at a 90-degree angle, and re-press the folds in the backing to hide the raw edges. Trim any excess fabric as necessary, and continue stitching around the corner and on to the next side. Carry on around the quilt until the full quilt is bound.

TIP
You can use pins or clips to easily keep your binding in place while you sew around the perimeter of your quilt. Pressing the folds with an iron can also be helpful.

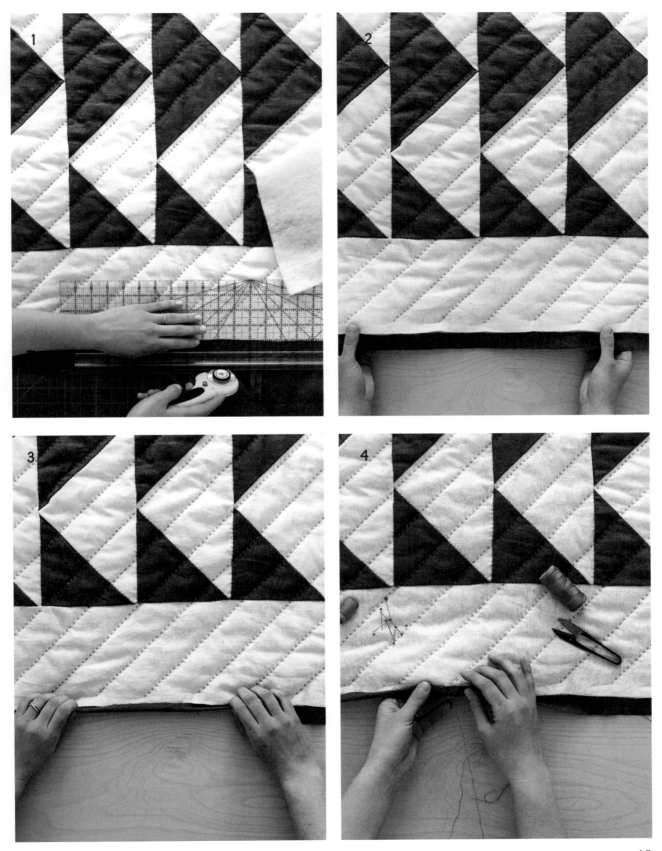

BIND WITH
BINDING STRIPS

To bind your quilt with binding strips, start by referring to the pattern, which will tell you how many binding strips to cut. Cut the appropriate number of strips, trim any selvedges and sew the strips end to end, with right sides together. Press the strip in half lengthways, wrong sides together. On one end, press the corner in at a right-angle about 2½in (7cm) from the edge, and then re-press the lengthways fold.

Position the binding strip, raw edges together, along the perimeter of your quilt, starting on one of the sides (not a corner). Sew the binding to the quilt with your sewing machine, stitching about 3–4in (8–10cm) in from the edge of the strip. (For this step, it's helpful to use a walking foot.)

When you reach a corner, backstitch ¼in (6mm) away from the edge and cut the thread. Flip the binding strip straight up and then back down again to form a mitred corner. Begin stitching ¼in (6mm) away from the edge, and continue around the perimeter of the quilt.

When you reach the end of your binding strip, trim away any excess and then insert the tail into the triangular fold you created earlier. Stitch the binding fully to the top of the quilt, backstitching to secure.

To finish the binding, wrap the folded edge of the binding strip around to the reverse side of the quilt and hand-stitch it down with a whipstitch, blind stitch, or stitch of your choice (see images 1 and 2). At the corners, fold the fabric over itself to form a mitred corner, and stitch in place (see images 3 and 4).

APPLIQUÉ

Place your appliqué fabric on top of the background fabric as indicated in the pattern. You can pin or glue in place, though I usually prefer not to. Tuck the edges of the appliqué fabric piece under about ⅛–¼in (3–6mm) and use a blind stitch or whipstitch to sew them to the background fabric (see images 1–3). Continue tucking the raw edges under and stitching in place until the fabric is fully affixed.

FINISHING CUSHIONS

1. On both envelope closures, press the long inner edge under to the wrong side by ¼in (6mm). Then turn it under by another ¼in (6mm) and press again. Topstitch to hem the closure. Place your quilted cushion top face up on your work surface. Align the raw edges of the envelope closures with the raw edges of the cushion top and pin in place.

2. Sew around the entire perimeter of the cushion using a ¼in (6mm) or ½in (12mm) seam for more stability. Trim the corners to reduce bulk.

3. Turn the cushion cover right side out through the opening in the envelope closure. Press seams and insert your cushion pad to finish.

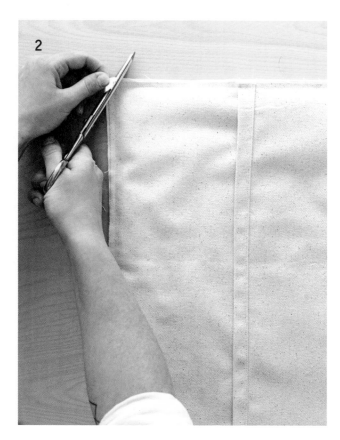

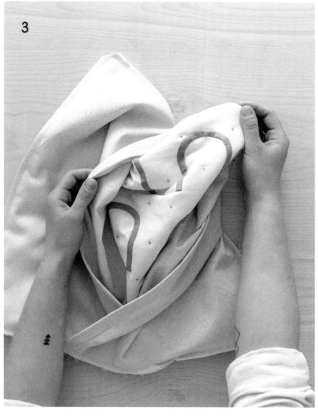

MAKING A THREAD BRAID

A thread braid is a simple and easy way to keep your threads neat and tidy when working with a skein, which is often how you'll find sashiko threads and some other high-contrast threads packaged. I use this method for all of my threads and have bins full of thread braids ready for any project.

1. Unwind your skein and locate a knot or loop where the loose ends are tied together. Hold this knot in one hand and position the thread in an oval shape with the knot furthest away from you.

2. Cut through the skein at the opposite end, furthest from the knot.

3. With the knot still opposite you, separate the strands into three equal sections.

4. Braid the sections by placing the right section over the middle, then the left over the middle, then the right, and so on.

5. When you reach the bottom of the braid, cut a small piece of thread from one strand.

6. Tie it around the braid to secure in place. To use the thread, pull a strand of thread out from the top of the braid near the knot. It is already cut into a convenient length for hand quilting, so now you're ready to sew!

QUILT CARE

A handmade quilt can last for generations with the right care. For the best results, it's useful to prewash your fabric before cutting, piecing and quilting (though not necessary). Prewashing will ensure your finished quilt doesn't shrink, and can reduce wrinkles and puckers. To prewash, simply throw your fabric in the wash before cutting and wash on a cool, gentle cycle. For the first wash, I recommend using a dye catcher to prevent any loose dye from bleeding onto other fabrics. Tumble dry your fabric on low heat. I recommend applying heat so any shrinking will occur before you make the quilt.

If you choose not to prewash, the first time you wash your quilt may change how the fabric looks and acts – wrinkles and puckers may appear and make the quilt look more lived in. However, in my experience, handmade quilts will continue to soften with age, time and washing, and each phase of its life can be more beautiful than the one before.

To wash your finished quilt, use a gentle wash cycle with cold water. Tumble dry on a low heat setting or hang to dry. Steaming a quilt is the best way to remove wrinkles, or you can use a hot iron with or without steam. Be sure to read the care instructions that come with your batting as care suggestions can vary with by brand and fibre content. (For example, wool batting can sometimes lose its loftiness when ironing, though it tends to puff back up in the wash.)

To store your quilts, I recommend folding into thirds and then rolling into a cylinder. Folding a quilt in the same area repeatedly can result in creases that can become permanent, so I recommend folding in different areas from time to time. Store your quilts away from direct sunlight to protect against fading. If rips or tears occur, you can hand sew the area closed with a thin, sturdy thread, or sew on a simple patch to mend the area.

Follow these tips, and your quilt can last for years and can be passed down to future generations. However, as one last note: my favourite thing about quilts is that they are beautiful and functional objects. So don't be afraid to use your quilts, get them dirty, take them on picnics, make blanket forts, and, of course, snuggle up with loved ones on a cosy evening (even if your company is prone to spills). Often the memories are worth the mess.

A NOTE ON PERFECTION

As you continue on your quilting journey, you may find that your work changes over time; your stitch length may get smaller or larger, or you may become more comfortable with a technique like hand piecing or sewing curves. Don't be too hard on yourself if your quilt looks different from how you envisioned it. Good things take practice, and there is no "perfect" in quilting – especially when it comes to handwork. Let go of any expectations for what your quilt should look like, and just enjoy the process and the way your work evolves.

For me, sometimes the length of my quilting stitches can even vary from when I begin a quilt to when I end it. I get more familiar with the materials, the weight of the quilt, the way my hands work with the specific motif, and that's okay. No line is perfectly straight, no stitch is the perfect width, and looking at a quilt from a distance often erases all the imperfections you may see when working up close. Embrace your unique sewing practice and the things that show your unique "hand of the maker".

HAND CARE

Handwork, while therapeutic for the soul, can pose physical challenges for the hands, so proper stretching and hand care will bring further joy and longevity to your practice. Take breaks from your handwork when you need to and find small ways to care for yourself. Thimbles can provide relief from pressure points on your fingers, and a rubber grip can make it easier to pull the needle through layers of fabric. And in addition to the hand exercises below, I love doing chest- and shoulder-opening stretches while sewing to care for my back and neck. At night, cuticle oil, hand lotion and essential oils can help to rejuvenate dry skin and also help you to sink deeper into a calm and relaxed state after a long stretch of handwork.

1. Massage the meaty part of your palm, near the thumb to release tension from holding the needle and thread. You can do this with the thumb of your opposite hand or a tennis ball or lacrosse ball.

2. Use the thumb of your opposite hand to massage the webbing between fingers and the muscles in your palm.

3. Gently stretch your fingers by pressing them together and rolling from side to side across your hand. Stretch the webbing between your thumb and index finger.

4. If you experience tension from trigger points in your forearms, use your thumb or a ball to gently massage the inside of your forearm below your elbow. You'll feel blood flow rush to your fingers as these muscles release.

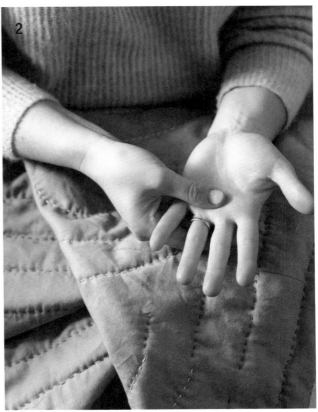

COMMUNITY QUILTING

Throughout history, handwork has not only brought joy in the form of a finished quilt that staves off the cold and brings comfort, but it has also provided a reason for women and makers to form communities when other opportunities to do so were scarce. Quilters came together to sew, forming sewing circles, guilds and bees. Sometimes they made individual blocks to be sewn together into a community quilt, or they would huddle under one large quilt, with each person hand-quilting a section.

Today, many hand quilters come together just for the company, forming sewing groups, attending retreats and enjoying the fellowship of other makers without the distraction of sewing machines. There's a reason that handwork is often referred to as "slow stitching" – quilting by hand somehow brings out the joy in the little things, and lets the distractions of the busy world around us fade away.

HOW TO MAKE A COMMUNITY QUILT

Below are some tips for making a community quilt by hand with others. Alternatively, you may want to form a sewing group and come together to make your own, unique projects. Whatever your goals, gather some friends together and enjoy quilting as a community.

FIND YOUR CREW
This can be a group of friends or family, or simply a community of quilters in your area. Invite expert quilters and beginners to be part of your group, so you can learn from each other, or work with others at your own skill level so you can practice together.

DIVIDE THE WORK
Decide how you'd like to share out the work. A block-based quilt, such as Monta (page 64), Pines (page 76), Likeness (page 162) or Ritual (page 168), lends itself well to assigning a number of blocks to each person – hand piecing can be especially fun to undertake as a group. For a large quilt, such as the king-size versions of Talus (page 100), Parlour (page 84) or Reflect (page 92), one or two people can piece the quilt and the group can help to quilt or tie the layers together. For small quilts, such as Centro (page 110), Union (page 148) or Lune (page 128), you may all want to make your own versions but meet up to stitch as a group. If you have a group of beginners, you could start with Steady (page 70), and invite everyone to sew a few rows or make their own version of the quilt.

MAKE A SCHEDULE AND SEW
Like a book club, it's fun to gather regularly to sew with your "quilt club". Maybe your group meets one weekend a month, or one night a week for several weeks. Choose how often you'd like to meet, and set goals for each session. A sample schedule might be:

Week 1: Meet and discuss fabric options
Week 2: Sew blocks
Week 3: Assemble the quilt top
Week 4: Mark and baste
Week 5: Quilt
Week 6: Bind and finish

HAVE FUN
Whatever shape your community quilt project takes, keep an open mind and have fun with likeminded makers. Some of my best friends are women I've met through quilting, and you'll always have an excuse to get together and sew.

►►► **THE
PROJECTS**
►►►►►

MONTA

An exercise in symmetry, this quilt has a design that reminds me of a reflection on water. Monta was inspired by the landscape of my home in Colorado, with tall peaks often rising up from and reflected in calm mountain lakes. The prospect of making this quilt in the larger size may seem daunting, but the big pieces come together quickly, and when it comes to quilting, the negative space leaves plenty of room for play and exploration, so maybe incorporate a new stitching motif you've been wanting to try. It's fun and adventurous, just like a day in the mountains.

SIZE	IMPERIAL	METRIC
Twin	70 x 90in	178 x 229cm

MATERIALS

The default instructions are written for wide fabric with a width of 54in or 137cm. Variations for standard-width fabric of 42in or 107cm are indicated in the table opposite and given in parentheses in the cutting instructions: Wide (Standard).

▶ Dark Fabric: Essex Ochre YD
▶ Light Fabric: Essex Ivory wide
▶ Backing: Brussels Washer Yarn-Dyed Redrock
▶ Binding: Essex Ivory wide
▶ Batting: Quilters Dream Wool

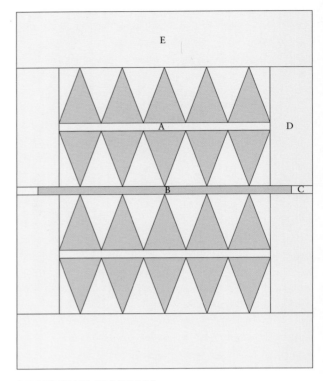

ASSEMBLY DIAGRAM

QUILTING GUIDE

TWIN

Fabric	Imperial		Metric	
	Standard (42in)	Wide (54in)	Standard (107cm)	Wide (137cm)
Dark	1⅝yd	1⅝yd	1.5m	1.5m
Light	5yd	4½yd	4.15m	4m
Backing	5½yd	4⅜yd	5.05m	4m
Batting	72 x 92in	72 x 92in	183 x 234cm	183 x 234cm
Binding	¾yd	⅝yd	70cm	60cm

CUTTING INSTRUCTIONS

From the Dark Fabric, cut:
▶ 3 (3) strips 15in x WOF. Subcut:
  ▶ 20 triangles using template
▶ 2 (2) strips 2½in x WOF. Subcut:
  ▶ 2 strips 2½ x 30½in (B)

From the Light Fabric, cut:
▶ 3 (4) strips 15in x WOF. Subcut:
  ▶ 24 triangles using template
▶ 4 (4) strips 14½in x WOF. Subcut:
  ▶ 4 strips 14½ x 35½in (E)
▶ 4 (4) strips 10½in x WOF. Subcut:
  ▶ 4 rectangles 10½ x 30½in (D)
▶ 3 (4) strips 2½in x WOF. Subcut:
  ▶ 2 strips 2½ x 50½in (A)
  (4 strips 2½ x 25½in)
  ▶ 2 rectangles 2½ x 5½in (C)

From the Backing Fabric, cut:
▶ Standard: 2 pieces 98in x WOF
▶ Wide: 2 pieces 78in x WOF

From the Batting, cut:
▶ 1 piece 72 x 92in (183 x 234cm)

From the Binding Fabric, cut:
▶ 7 (9) strips 2½in x WOF

SEWING INSTRUCTIONS

1. Sew pairs of the following strips together, end to end, to form border strips of the appropriate size.

	Pieced strip size	Number of pieced strips
A*	2½ x 50½in	2
B	2½ x 60½in	1
E	14½ x 70½in	2

* Standard-width fabric only

ASSEMBLE THE TRIANGLE ROWS

2. Sew together six light triangles and five
    dark triangles, as shown, to create a row
    (Diagram 1). Using an iron, press the seams
    open and trim the edges to square it up to
    approximately 50½ x 14½in. Repeat to
    make a total of four rows of triangles.

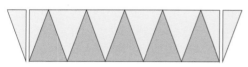

Diagram 1

3. Sew two rows of triangles together with an A
    strip between them (Diagram 2). Press the seams
    open. Then sew a D rectangle to both ends of the
    row, pressing the seams open. Repeat to make
    a second triangle centre unit.

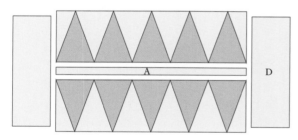

Diagram 2

4. Sew the two C rectangles to either end of the
    B strip, as shown, to make a middle strip
    (Diagram 3). Press the seams open.

Diagram 3

5. Sew the triangle centre units together with
    the middle strip between them. Then join the
    E rectangles to the top and bottom as shown
    (Diagram 4). Press the seams open to finish
    the quilt top.

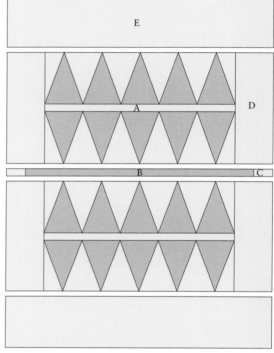

Diagram 4

ASSEMBLING THE QUILT

Refer to pages 36–51 for assembling, quilting and
binding your quilt. Turn to page 66 for the assembly
diagram and quilting guide.

QUILTING SUGGESTIONS

To finish your quilt like the one pictured, mark your
quilting lines as follows:

▶ Beginning in the centre of the quilt, mark diagonal
lines parallel to the lines of the triangles about
3–6½in (8–17cm) apart. Extend the lines to the
edges of the quilt.

TIP

Mark your first lines at a ¼in margin on either side of
the two most central triangles. Use these as anchoring
lines from which to mark additional lines as you
move outwards.

STEADY

Every quilter should have a go-to design – one that they love to make, that can be sewn into a quick gift or that can pick them out of a creative rut with some good, old-fashioned sewing that's easy and enjoyable. The Steady quilt is exactly that for me. It was the first quilt I made in my new home, because it's just plain fun to put together. It's a great quilt for beginners, but it is a satisfying make for more seasoned quilters, too. Since it's made with width-of-fabric strips, you can cut, sew and complete this quilt top in a day or a weekend. Then enjoy some slow stitching as you hand quilt this beauty in your own unique style.

SIZE	IMPERIAL	METRIC
Throw	59½ x 66in	151 x 168cm

This pattern can easily be scaled up or down to suit your needs. To learn more about scaling, please see Scaling Patterns on page 24.

SCALING SUGGESTIONS

▶ *Queen:* Scale up by 150 per cent to make a quilt that finishes at 90 x 99in or 229 x 252cm
▶ *Baby:* Scale down by 50 per cent to make a quilt that finishes at 30 x 33in or 76 x 84cm

MATERIALS

This pattern works best when using wide fabric (at least 54in or 137cm). If you would like to use standard-width fabric (42in or 107cm), I recommend scaling down and making the cot-size quilt. The default instructions are written for wide fabric with a width of 54in or 137cm.

▶ Dark Fabric: Essex Natural wide
▶ Light Fabric: Essex Ivory wide
▶ Backing: Essex Ivory wide
▶ Binding: Essex Ivory wide
▶ Batting: Quilters Dream Wool

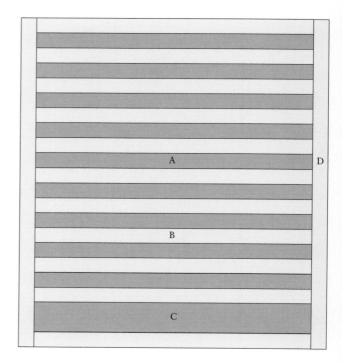

ASSEMBLY DIAGRAM

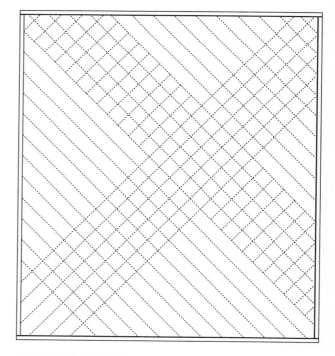

QUILTING GUIDE

THROW

Fabric	Imperial Wide (54in)	Metric Wide (137cm)
Dark	1¼yd	1.15m
Light	1⅝yd	1.5m
Backing	3⅞yd	3.55m
Batting	61½ x 68in	156 x 173cm
Binding	½yd	50cm

CUTTING INSTRUCTIONS

From the Dark Fabric, cut:
▶ 1 strip 6½in x WOF. Subcut:
  ▶ 1 strip 6½ x 54in (C)
▶ 9 strips 3½in x WOF. Subcut:
  ▶ 9 strips 3½ x 54in (A)

From the Light Fabric, cut:
▶ 15 strips 3½in x WOF. Subcut:
  ▶ 11 strips 3½ x 54in (B)
  ▶ 4 strips 3½ x 33½in (D)

From the Backing Fabric, cut:
▶ 2 pieces 69in x WOF

From the Batting, cut:
▶ 61½ x 68in (156 x 173cm)

From the Binding Fabric, cut:
▶ 5 strips 2½in x WOF

SEWING INSTRUCTIONS

ASSEMBLE THE QUILT TOP

1. Sew nine A and ten B strips together as shown, pressing the seams open with an iron as you go (Diagram 1).

Diagram 1

2. Sew the C strip to the bottom of your quilt top, as shown, and press the seam open (Diagram 2). Then sew the final B strip to the bottom of the C strip and press the seam open.

4. Sew one D strip to the right side of your quilt top and one D strip to the left of your quilt top as shown (Diagram 3). Press the seams open to finish the quilt top.

Diagram 2

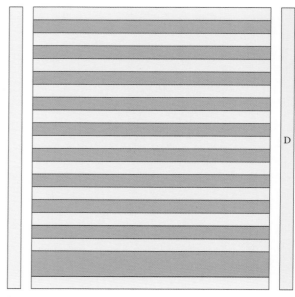

Diagram 3

3. Sew two D strips together, end to end, to make a strip 3½ x 66½in long. Repeat with the remaining two D strips to make a second strip 3½ x 66½in long. Press all the seams open.

ASSEMBLING THE QUILT

Refer to pages 36–51 for assembling, quilting and binding your quilt. Turn to page 72 for the assembly diagram and quilting guide.

QUILTING SUGGESTIONS

To finish your quilt like the one pictured, mark your quilting lines as follows:

▶ Using the 45-degree line on your quilting ruler, mark intersecting diagonal lines 3in (8cm) apart in an X-shape through your quilt (I put the X in my quilt off to one side).

▶ Continue marking 45-degree lines 3in (8cm) apart in the background surrounding the X to extend quilting throughout the quilt.

PINES

I was born in Colorado and lived there during my early childhood, before moving to Wyoming, then to Iowa as a young adult. I am proud of all my homes, but returning to Colorado with my husband has been an opportunity to build a new home for ourselves. The mountains were one of the main reasons we chose to settle here – they have always inspired me, and I feel at home up high among the sea of pine trees. I chose to hand piece this quilt, partly because the bias edges come together more easily with a little more attention, and partly because I just wanted to sit with it a little longer.

SIZE	IMPERIAL	METRIC
Twin	72 x 75in	183 x 191cm
Baby	24 x 25in	61 x 64cm

MATERIALS

The default instructions are written for wide fabric with a width of 54in or 137cm. Variations for standard-width fabric of 42in or 107cm are indicated in the table opposite and given in parentheses in the cutting instructions: Wide (Standard).

▶ Dark Fabric: Brussels Washer O.D. Green
▶ Light Fabric: Essex Ivory wide
▶ Backing: Brussels Washer O.D. Green
▶ Binding: Essex Ivory wide
▶ Batting: Quilters Dream Wool

ASSEMBLY DIAGRAM

QUILTING GUIDE

TWIN

Fabric	Imperial Standard (42in)	Wide (54in)	Metric Standard (107cm)	Wide (137cm)
Dark	2¼yd	1⅞yd	2.05m	1.75m
Light	3⅞yd	3⅜yd	3.55m	3.1m
Backing	4½yd	4½yd	4.15m	4.15m
Batting	74 x 77in	74 x 77in	188 x 196cm	188 x 196cm
Binding	⅝yd	½yd	60cm	50cm

CUTTING INSTRUCTIONS

From the Dark Fabric, cut:
▶ 4 (5) strips 13in x WOF. Subcut:
  ▶ 15 squares 13 x 13in

From the Light Fabric, cut:
▶ 4 (5) strips 13in x WOF. Subcut:
  ▶ 13 squares 13 x 13in
▶ 2 (2) strips 9½in x WOF. Subcut:
  ▶ 2 strips 9½ x 30½in (bottom border)
▶ 6 (6) strips 6½in x WOF. Subcut:
  ▶ 4 strips 6½ x 38in (left and right borders)
  ▶ 2 strips 6½ x 30½in (top border)

From the Backing Fabric, cut:
▶ 2 pieces 80in x WOF

From the Batting, cut:
▶ 1 piece 74 x 77in (188 x 196cm)

From the Binding Fabric, cut:
▶ 6 (8) strips 2½in wide

BABY

Fabric	Imperial Standard (42in)	Wide (54in)	Metric Standard (107cm)	Wide (137cm)
Dark	⅜yd	⅜yd	35cm	35cm
Light	⅔yd	⅝yd	65cm	60cm
Backing	1yd	1yd	95cm	95cm
Batting	26 x 27in	26 x 27in	66 x 69cm	66 x 69cm
Binding	⅜yd	¼yd	35cm	25cm

CUTTING INSTRUCTIONS

From the Dark Fabric, cut:
▶ 2 (2) strips 5in x WOF. Subcut:
  ▶ 15 squares 5 x 5in

From the Light Fabric, cut:
▶ 2 (2) strips 5in x WOF. Subcut:
  ▶ 13 squares 5 x 5in
▶ 1 (1) strip 3½in x WOF. Subcut:
  ▶ 1 strip 3½ x 20½in (bottom border)
▶ 2 (3) strips 2½in x WOF. Subcut:
  ▶ 2 strips 2½ x 25½in (left and right borders)
  ▶ 1 strip 2½ x 20½in (top border)

From the Backing fabric, cut:
▶ 1 piece 30in x WOF

From the Batting, cut:
▶ 1 piece 26 x 27in (66 x 69cm)

From the Binding Fabric, cut:
▶ 2 (3) strips 2½in wide

SEWING INSTRUCTIONS

PREPARE THE PIECES

1. Subcut the light and dark squares across both diagonals, as shown, to create four triangles from each square (Diagram 1). Subcutting will yield 60 dark and 52 light triangles. Set aside two light triangles for a future project, reserving 50 for this quilt.

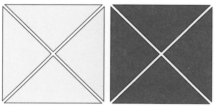

Diagram 1

2. For the twin size only, sew two of the following strips together end to end to form border strips of the appropriate size.

	Pieced strip size	*Number of pieced strips*
Bottom border	9½ x 60½in	1
Left and right borders	6½ x 75½in	2
Top border	6½ x 60½in	1

ASSEMBLE THE ROWS

3. Arrange a light and dark triangle with right sides together as shown (Diagram 2). Pin in place and sew together with a ¼in seam allowance. Using an iron, press the seam open.

¼in

¼in

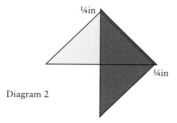

Diagram 2

4. In the same way, sew together a total of five light triangles and six dark triangles to create a full row (Diagram 3). Press the seams open and trim both ends to square up the row as shown. Repeat to make a total of ten rows.

Diagram 3

5. Sew the rows together as shown (Diagram 4). Press the seams open.

Diagram 4

6. Sew the top and bottom borders to the quilt top and press the seams open (Diagram 5).

Diagram 5

7. Sew the left and right borders to the quilt top and press the seams open to finish (Diagram 6).

Diagram 6

ASSEMBLING THE QUILT

Refer to pages 36–51 for assembling, quilting and binding your quilt. Turn to page 78 for the assembly diagram and quilting guide.

QUILTING SUGGESTIONS

To finish your quilt like the one pictured, mark your quilting lines as follows:

▶ Beginning in the centre, mark lines parallel to the angles of the flying-geese blocks in 2in (5cm) increments. Allow the lines to cross in the centre. At the edges of the quilt, instead of intersecting the lines as they come together, allow the stitching to come together at right angles.

PARLOUR

Everything about this quilt is joyful, and I have to admit
that it's one of my favourites. Built completely with curved
blocks, it's a good one to make entirely by hand. Once I had
finished this quilt top, I decided to tie the quilt with French
knots to add a light, whimsical texture. Hand quilting should
be enjoyable, first and foremost, and I encourage you to make
thoughtful choices at each stage to create pleasure in the
process. The arches in the quilt reminded me of a grand house
with a beautiful entrance and large doorways that welcome
guests to come inside, to sit and stay a while. The boundaries
are so thin, they're almost not there at all, and they remind me
of the pleasure of hosting company and keeping an open door
for friends, family and neighbours.

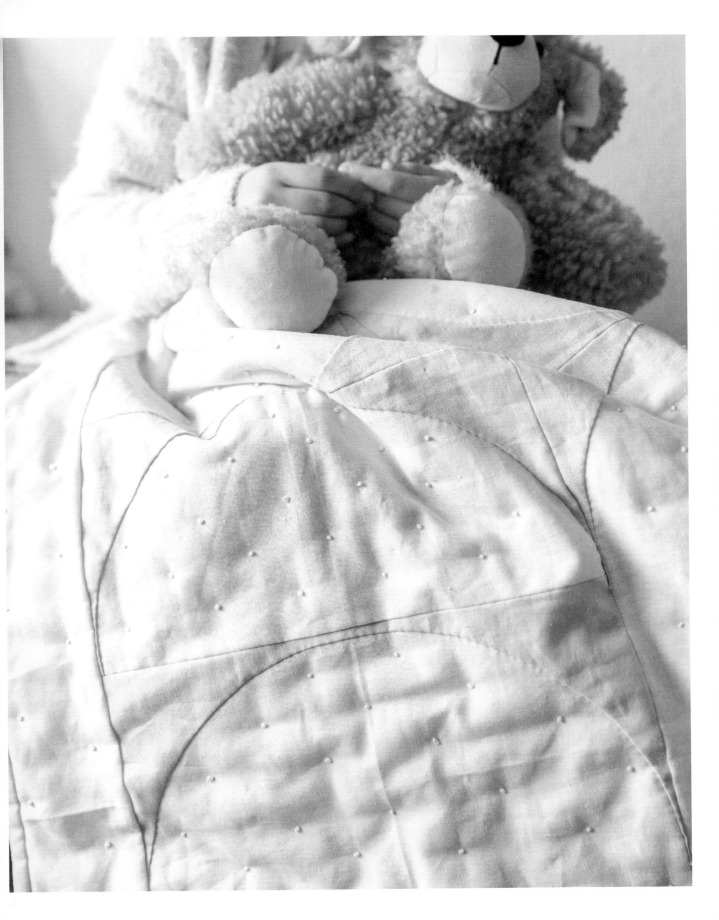

SIZE	IMPERIAL	METRIC
Queen	72 x 84in	183 x 213cm
Baby	36 x 42in	91 x 107cm

MATERIALS

The default instructions are written for standard-width fabric of 42in or 107cm. Variations for wide fabric with a width of 54in or 137cm are indicated in the table and given in parentheses in the cutting instructions: Wide (Standard).

▶ Dark Fabric: Essex Peach
▶ Light Fabric: Essex Ivory wide
▶ Backing: Essex Ivory wide
▶ Binding: Essex Ivory wide
▶ Batting: Quilters Dream Wool

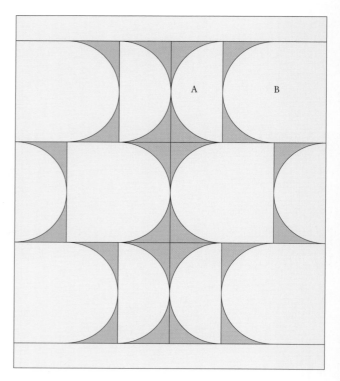

ASSEMBLY DIAGRAM

QUILTING GUIDE

QUEEN

Fabric	Imperial Standard (42in)	Wide (54in)	Metric Standard (107cm)	Wide (137cm)
Dark	3yd	2¼yd	2.75m	2.1m
Light	5½yd	4⅝yd	5.05m	4.25m
Backing	5yd	5yd	4.6m	4.6m
Batting	74 x 86in	74 x 86in	188 x 218cm	188 x 218cm
Binding	⅝yd	⅝yd	60cm	60cm

CUTTING INSTRUCTIONS

From the Dark Fabric, cut:
▶ 4 (3) strips 26in x WOF. Subcut:
  ▶ 12 rectangles 26 x 13½in

From the Light Fabric, cut:
▶ 6 (5) strips 25in x WOF. Subcut:
  ▶ 6 squares 25 x 25in (B)
  ▶ 6 rectangles 25 x 13in (A)
▶ 4 (4) strips 6½in x WOF. Subcut:
  ▶ 4 strips 6½ x 36½in (borders)

From the Backing Fabric, cut:
▶ 2 pieces 90in x WOF

From the Batting, cut:
▶ 1 piece 74 x 86in (188 x 218cm)

From the Binding Fabric, cut:
▶ 8 (7) strips 2½in x WOF

BABY

Fabric	Imperial Standard (42in)	Wide (54in)	Metric Standard (107cm)	Wide (137cm)
Dark	1yd	⅔yd	95cm	65cm
Light	1⅓yd	1⅓yd	1.25m	1.25m
Backing	1⅜yd	1¼yd	1.3m	1.2m
Batting	38 x 44in	38 x 44in	97 x 112cm	97 x 112cm
Binding	½yd	⅜yd	50cm	35cm

CUTTING INSTRUCTIONS

From the Dark Fabric, cut:
▶ 4 (3) strips 6¾in x WOF. Subcut:
  ▶ 12 rectangles 6¾ x 13in

From the Light Fabric, cut:
▶ 3 (3) strips 12½in x WOF. Subcut:
  ▶ 6 squares 12½ x 12½in (B)
  ▶ 6 rectangles 12½ x 6½in (A)
▶ 2 (2) strips 3½in x WOF. Subcut:
  ▶ 2 (2) strips 3½ x 36½in (borders)

From the Backing Fabric, cut:
▶ Standard: 49in x WOF
▶ Wide: 45in x WOF

From the Batting, cut:
▶ 1 piece 38 x 44in (97 x 112 cm)

From the Binding Fabric, cut:
▶ 5 (4) strips 2½in x WOF

SEWING INSTRUCTIONS

PREPARE THE TEMPLATES AND PIECES

1. Download and print the templates from riane-elise.com/quilting-by-hand.

2. If you are making the queen size, sew two border strips end to end to make a strip 6½ x 72½in. Using an iron, press the seam open. Repeat to make a second border strip.

3. Take the dark rectangles – 26 x 13½in for the queen or 13 x 6¾in for the baby – and press them in half widthways. Likewise, press the light A and light B pieces in half widthways. The A pieces should end up nearly square and the B pieces should end up in a long, rectangular shape (Diagram 1). Leave them folded for the next step.

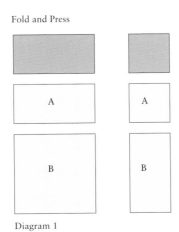

Fold and Press

Diagram 1

4. Align the edge of the convex template with the folded edge of the light A piece as shown (Diagram 2). Trace the curve on the fabric. Cut along your marked line and reserve the half circle. Mark the centre top for future reference (Diagram 3). Repeat to make at total of six convex A pieces.

Diagram 2

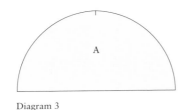

Diagram 3

5. Align the edge of the convex template with the top corner of the folded edge of the light B piece as shown (Diagram 4). Trace the curve on the fabric and mark the fabric at the bottom of the template for future reference. Cut along your marked line, mark the centre top and reserve the curved shape (Diagram 5). Repeat to make a total of six convex B pieces.

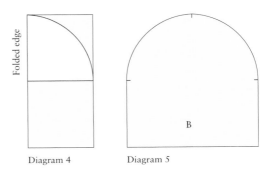

Diagram 4   Diagram 5

6. Align the edge of the concave template with the folded edge of the dark fabric as shown (Diagram 6). Trace the curve on the fabric. Cut along your marked line and reserve the outer shape. Mark the centre for future reference (Diagram 7). Repeat to make a total of 12 concave dark pieces.

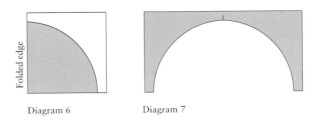

Diagram 6   Diagram 7

TIP

When cutting out the pieces, use a few pins on either side of your marked line to hold the folded layers together. This makes for a nice, clean cut.

SEW THE CURVED PIECES

7. Refer to Sewing Curves on page 33. Using your preferred method, mark, align, pin and sew the convex and concave A curves together, making a total of six A rectangles. For the B pieces, line up the bottom edges of the dark piece with the marks you made in Step 5 to indicate the bottom of the convex template (Diagram 8). Sew the convex and concave B pieces together making a total of six B squares. Press the seams towards the concave (dark) fabric.

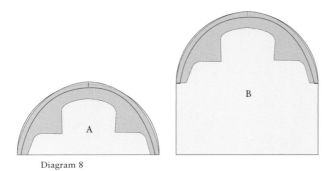

Diagram 8

8. Trim the A rectangles to 12½ x 24½in for the queen, or 6½ x 12½in for the baby, making sure to leave ¼in on the sides and top of the curve (Diagram 9).

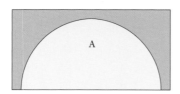

Diagram 9

9. Trim the B squares to 24½ x 24½in for the queen, or 12½ x 12½in for the baby, making sure to leave ¼in on the sides and top of the curve (Diagram 10).

Diagram 10

ASSEMBLE THE QUILT TOP

10. Sew two A rectangles and two B squares together in a row as shown (Diagram 11). Press the seams towards the dark fabric. Repeat Step 10 to make a second row in the same configuration.

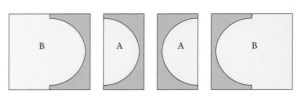

Diagram 11

11. Sew two A rectangles and two B squares together in a row as shown (Diagram 12). Press the seams towards the light fabric.

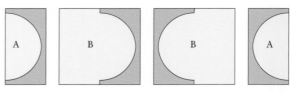

Diagram 12

12. Sew the rows together as shown (Diagram 13). Press the seams open.

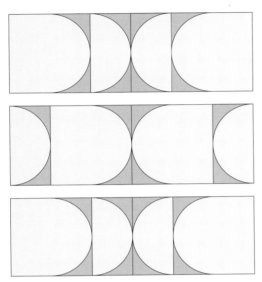

Diagram 13

13. Sew the two borders to the top and bottom of the quilt top (Diagram 14). Press the seams open to finish.

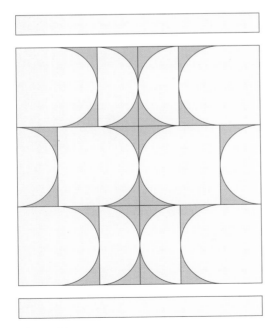

Diagram 14

ASSEMBLING THE QUILT
Refer to pages 36–51 for assembling, quilting and binding your quilt. Turn to page 86 for the assembly diagram and quilting guide.

QUILTING SUGGESTIONS
To finish your quilt like the one pictured, mark your quilting lines as follows:

▶ Mark small staggered dots every 2–2½in (5–7cm) throughout the quilt.

▶ Use the dots as markers for where to place each French knot.

REFLECT

I find so much beauty in simplicity, and the most straightforward designs remind me that a strong and simple foundation is really all we need; the rest is what we choose to make of it. Reflect is a simple quilt, made of nothing more than strips and straight lines, but the quilting adds another layer of visual interest. I love how the piecing and quilting elements play together beautifully to create something special.

SIZE	IMPERIAL	METRIC
Queen	80 x 96in	203 x 244cm
Baby	40 x 48in	102 x 122cm

MATERIALS

The default instructions are written for wide fabric with a width of 54in or 137cm. Variations for standard-width fabric of 42in or 107cm are indicated in the table opposite and given in parentheses in the cutting instructions: Wide (Standard).

▶ Dark Fabric: Essex Leather
▶ Light Fabric: Essex Natural wide
▶ Backing: Brussels Washer O.D. Green
▶ Binding: Essex Leather
▶ Batting: Quilters Dream Wool

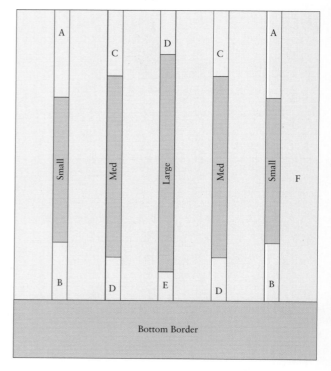

ASSEMBLY DIAGRAM

QUILTING GUIDE

QUEEN

Fabric	Imperial Standard (42in)	Wide (54in)	Metric Standard (107cm)	Wide (137cm)
Dark	2⅛yd	2⅛yd	1.95m	1.95m
Light	4½yd	4¼yd	4.15m	3.9m
Backing	7⅓yd	5yd	6.75m	4.6m
Batting	82 x 98in	82 x 98in	208 x 249cm	208 x 249cm
Binding	¾yd	⅝yd	70cm	60cm

CUTTING INSTRUCTIONS

From the Dark Fabric, cut:
- ▶ 2 (2) strips 16½in x WOF. Subcut:
  - ▶ 2 strips 16½ x 40½in (bottom border)
- ▶ 8 (8) strips 4½in x WOF. Subcut:
  - ▶ 2 strips 4½ x 40½in (small)
  - ▶ 2 rectangles 4½ x 30½in (H – forms one large strip)
  - ▶ 4 rectangles 4½ x 25½in (G – forms two medium strips)

From the Light Fabric, cut:
- ▶ 12 (12) strips 10½in x WOF. Subcut:
  - ▶ 12 rectangles 10½ x 40½in (F)
- ▶ 4 (5) strips 4½in x WOF. Subcut:
  - ▶ 2 rectangles 4½ x 24½in (A)
  - ▶ 2 rectangles 4½ x 16½in (B)
  - ▶ 2 rectangles 4½ x 18½in (C)
  - ▶ 3 rectangles 4½ x 12½in (D)
  - ▶ 1 rectangle 4½ x 8½in (E)

From the Backing Fabric, cut:
- ▶ Standard: 3 pieces 88in x WOF
- ▶ Wide: 2 pieces 90in x WOF

From the Batting, cut:
- ▶ 1 piece 82 x 98in (208 x 249cm)

From the Binding Fabric, cut:
- ▶ 7 (9) strips 2½in x WOF

BABY

Fabric	Imperial Standard (42in)	Wide (54in)	Metric Standard (107cm)	Wide (137cm)
Dark	⅝yd	½yd	60cm	50cm
Light	1¼yd	1¼yd	1.15m	1.15m
Backing	2⅔yd	1⅝yd	2.45m	1.5m
Batting	42 x 50in	42 x 50in	107 x 127cm	107 x 127cm
Binding	½yd	⅜yd	50cm	35cm

CUTTING INSTRUCTIONS

From the Dark Fabric, cut:
- ▶ 1 (1) strip 8½in x WOF. Subcut:
  - ▶ 1 strip 8½ x 40½in (bottom border)
- ▶ 3 (4) strips 2½in x WOF. Subcut:
  - ▶ 1 strip 2½ x 30½in (large)
  - ▶ 2 strips 2½ x 25½in (medium)
  - ▶ 2 strips 2½ x 20½in (small)

From the Light Fabric, cut:
- ▶ 6 (6) strips 5½in x WOF. Subcut:
  - ▶ 6 strips 5½ x 40½in (F)
- ▶ 2 (3) strips 2½in x WOF. Subcut:
  - ▶ 2 rectangles 2½ x 12½in (A)
  - ▶ 2 rectangles 2½ x 8½in (B)
  - ▶ 2 rectangles 2½ x 9½in (C)
  - ▶ 3 rectangles 2½ x 6½in (D)
  - ▶ 1 rectangle 2½ x 4½in (E)

From the Backing Fabric, cut:
- ▶ Standard: 2 pieces 48in x WOF
- ▶ Wide: 1 piece 48 x 56in x WOF

From the Batting, cut:
- ▶ 1 piece 42 x 50in (104 x 124cm)

From the Binding Fabric, cut:
- ▶ 4 (5) strips 2½in x WOF

SEWING INSTRUCTIONS

PREPARE THE PIECES (QUEEN SIZE ONLY)

1. Sew pairs of the following pieces together, end to end, to form strips of the appropriate strip size. Skip this step if you are making the baby size.

	Pieced strip size	*Number of pieced strips*
G rectangles (Med)	4½ x 50½in	2
H rectangles (Large)	4½ x 60½in	1
F rectangles	10½ x 80½in	6
Bottom border	16½ x 80½in	1

ASSEMBLE THE STRIPS

2. Sew an A rectangle to the right-hand end of a dark small strip and a B rectangle to the left-hand end (Diagram 1). Using an iron, press the seams open and set aside. Repeat to make a second small strip.

B	Small	A

Diagram 1

TIP

As you finish each strip, press it in half widthways and mark the centre with a small mark on the wrong side. This will help you to line up the centre of the strips when you assemble the quilt top.

3. Sew a C rectangle to the right-hand end of a dark medium strip, and a D rectangle to the left-hand end (Diagram 2). Press the seams open and set aside. Repeat to make a second medium strip.

D	Medium	C

Diagram 2

4. Sew a D rectangle to the right-hand end of a dark large strip, and an E rectangle to the left-hand end (Diagram 3). Press the seams open and set aside.

Diagram 3

TIP

When assembling the strips, it's helpful to label the top of each strip. The A, C and D pieces (the right sides in Diagrams 1–3) will be at the top in the final quilt construction.

ASSEMBLE THE QUILT TOP

5. Sew the small, medium and large strips together with F strips in between (Diagram 4). Pay attention to the orientation of the strips as you sew. Press the seams open.

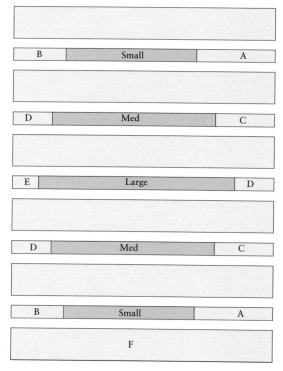

Diagram 4

TIP

When sewing long seams, it is helpful to pin seams together with straight pins.

6. Sew the bottom border strip to the bottom of the quilt top (Diagram 5). Press the seam open to finish the quilt top.

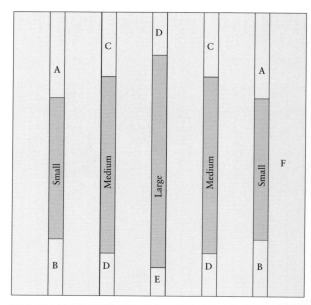

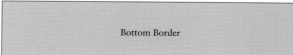

Diagram 5

ASSEMBLING THE QUILT

Refer to pages 36–51 for assembling, quilting and binding your quilt. Turn to page 94 for the assembly diagram and quilting guide.

QUILTING SUGGESTIONS

To finish your quilt like the one pictured, mark your quilting lines as follows:

▶ Align the 60-degree angle on your quilting ruler with the edge of one of the vertical rectangles in the quilt. Mark 60-degree lines 2in (5cm) throughout the centre of the quilt. Stop marking about 25-30in (64-75cm) from the opposing corners of the quilt, switch directions, and mark lines at a 60 degree angle from the lines you previously marked.

TALUS

If I were to choose a perfect bed quilt, this just might be it. Out of the countless quilts I've made, I hadn't yet made one for my own bed, but this was designed for that very reason. This design is the perfect mix of strong and subtle, making the bedroom feel safe and cosy – the perfect sanctuary. Talus also has instructions for a throw size, and it's just as sweet in a living room or office. For special quilts such as this, I like to think of the handwork process as infusing extra love and care into a quilt, making it that much more meaningful for those who use it.

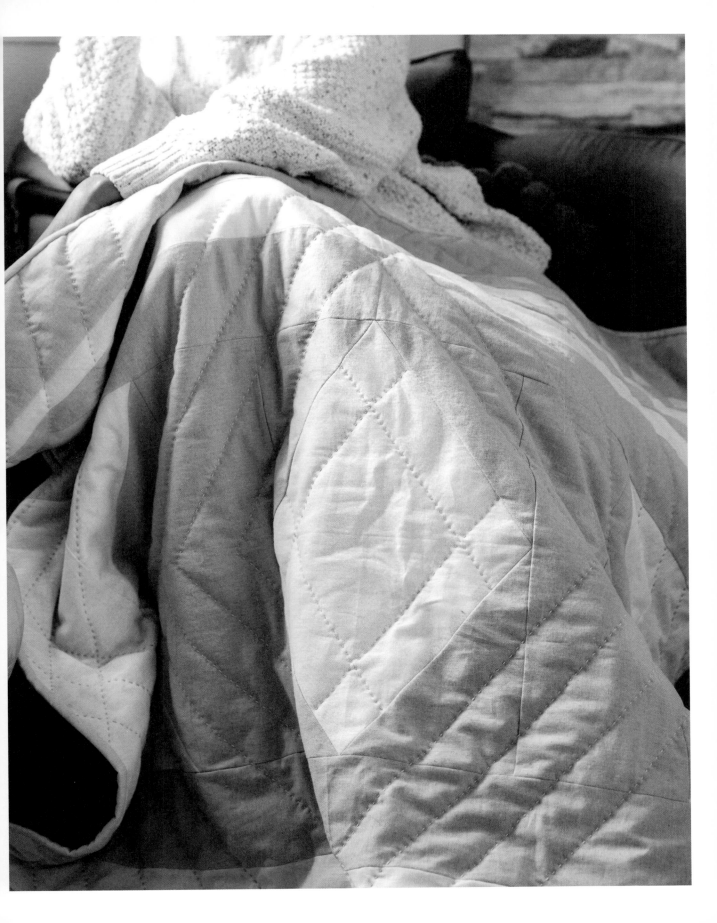

SIZE	IMPERIAL	METRIC
King	96 x 100in	244 x 254cm
Throw	48 x 50in	122 x 127cm

MATERIALS

The default instructions are written for wide fabric with a width of 54in or 137cm. Variations for standard-width fabric of 42in or 107cm are indicated in the table opposite and given in parentheses in the cutting instructions: Wide (Standard).

▶ Dark Fabric: Essex Natural wide
▶ Light Fabric: Essex Ivory wide
▶ Backing: Brussels Washer O.D. Green
▶ Binding: Essex Natural wide
▶ Batting: Quilters Dream Wool

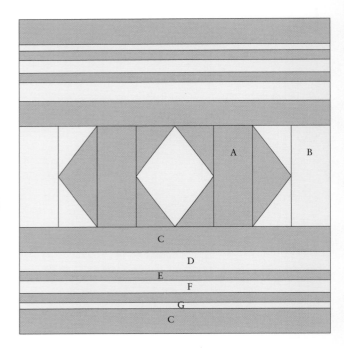

ASSEMBLY DIAGRAM

QUILTING GUIDE

KING

Fabric	Imperial Standard (42in)	Wide (54in)	Metric Standard (107cm)	Wide (137cm)
Dark	6½yd	5¼yd	5.95m	4.8m
Light	4¾yd	4yd	4.35m	3.65m
Backing	8¾yd	5⅞yd	8m	5.4m
Batting	98 x 102in	98 x 102in	249 x 259cm	249 x 259cm
Binding	⅞yd	⅝yd	80cm	50cm

NOTE

Two of the blocks in this quilt are based on the traditional flying geese block, which is a triangle (goose) surrounded by background fabric (referred to here as "sky").

CUTTING INSTRUCTIONS

From the Dark Fabric, cut:
▶ 4 (4) strips 12¾in x WOF. Subcut:
  ▸ 2 rectangles 12¾ x 32¾in (flying geese)
  ▸ 4 rectangles 12¾ x 16¾in (geese sky)
▶ 2 (2) strips 12½in x WOF. Subcut:
  ▸ 2 rectangles 12½ x 32½in (A)
▶ 8 (12) strips 8½in x WOF. Subcut:
  ▸ 8 strips 8½ x 48½in (C) (12 strips 8½ x 32½in)
▶ 8 (12) strips 3½in x WOF. Subcut:
  ▸ 8 strips 3½ x 48½in (E) (12 strips 3½ x 32½in)

From the Light Fabric, cut:
▶ 1 (1) strip 24¾in x WOF. Subcut:
  ▸ 1 rectangle 24¾ x 32¾in (diamond)
▶ 2 (2) strips 12¾in x WOF. Subcut:
  ▸ 4 rectangles 12¾ x 16¾in (geese sky)
▶ 2 (2) strips 12½in x WOF. Subcut:
  ▸ 2 rectangles 12½ x 32½in (B)
▶ 4 (6) strips 6½in x WOF. Subcut:
  ▸ 4 strips 6½ x 48½in (D) (6 strips 6½ x 32½in)
▶ 4 (6) strips 4½in x WOF. Subcut:
  ▸ 4 strips 4½ x 48½in (F) (6 strips 4½ x 32½in)
▶ 4 (6) strips 2½in x WOF. Subcut:
  ▸ 4 strips 2½ x 48½in (G) (6 strips 2½ x 32½in)

From the Backing Fabric, cut:
▶ Standard: 3 pieces 105in x WOF
▶ Wide: 2 pieces 105in x WOF

From the Batting Fabric, cut:
▶ 1 piece 98 x 102in (249 x 259cm)

From the Binding Fabric, cut:
▶ 8 (10) strips 2½in wide

THROW

Fabric	Imperial		Metric	
	Standard (42in)	Wide (54in)	Standard (107cm)	Wide (137cm)
Dark	2¼yd	1½yd	2.05m	1.4m
Light	1¾yd	1⅜yd	1.6m	1.25m
Backing	3¼yd	1⅝yd	3m	1.5m
Batting	50 x 52in	50 x 52in	127 x 132cm	127 x 132cm
Binding	½yd	⅜yd	50cm	35cm

CUTTING INSTRUCTIONS

From the Dark Fabric, cut:
- ▶ 2 (2) strips 6¾in x WOF. Subcut:
  - ▶ 2 rectangles 6¾ x 16 ¾in (flying geese)
  - ▶ 4 rectangles 6¾ x 8¾in (geese sky)
- ▶ 1 (1) strip 6½in x WOF. Subcut:
  - ▶ 2 rectangles 6½ x 16½in (A)
- ▶ 4 (8) strips 4½in x WOF. Subcut:
  - ▶ 4 strips 4½ x 48½in (C) (8 strips 4½ x 24½in)
- ▶ 4 (8) strips 2in x WOF. Subcut:
  - ▶ 4 strips 2 x 48½in (E) (8 strips 2 x 24½in)

From the Light Fabric, cut:
- ▶ 1 (1) strip 12¾in x WOF. Subcut:
  - ▶ 1 rectangle 12¾ x 16¾in (diamond)
- ▶ 1 (1) strip 6¾in x WOF. Subcut:
  - ▶ 4 rectangles 6¾ x 8¾in (geese sky)
- ▶ 1 (1) strip 6½in x WOF. Subcut:
  - ▶ 2 rectangles 6½ x 16½in (B)
- ▶ 2 (4) strips 3½in x WOF. Subcut:
  - ▶ 2 strips 3½ x 48½in (D) (4 strips 3½ x 24½in)
- ▶ 2 (4) strips 2½in x WOF. Subcut:
  - ▶ 2 strips 2½ x 48½in (F) (4 strips 2½ x 24½in)
- ▶ 2 (4) strips 1½in x WOF. Subcut:
  - ▶ 2 strips 1½ x 48½in (G) (4 strips 1½ x 24½in)

From the Backing Fabric, cut:
- ▶ Standard: 2 pieces 58in x WOF
- ▶ Wide: 1 piece 58in x WOF

From the Batting, cut:
- ▶ 1 piece 50 x 52in (127 x 132cm)

From the Binding Fabric, cut:
- ▶ 4 (6) strips 2½in wide

SEWING INSTRUCTIONS

PREPARE THE TEMPLATES AND PIECES

1. Download and print out the template for your chosen quilt size from riane-elise.com/quilting-by-hand and cut it out along the solid lines.

1. Sew two (or three, if you're using standard-width fabric) of the following strips together, end to end, to form pieces of the appropriate size.

KING

	Pieced strip size	Number of pieced strips
Dark C Strips	8½ x 96½in	4
Dark E Strips	3½ x 96½in	4
Light D Strips	6½ x 96½in	2
Light F Strips	4½ x 96½in	2
Light G Strips	2½ x 96½in	2

THROW (standard-width fabric only)

	Pieced strip size	Number of pieced strips
Dark C Strips	4½ x 48½in	4
Dark E Strips	2 x 48½in	4
Light D Strips	3½ x 48½in	2
Light F Strips	2½ x 48½in	2
Light G Strips	1½ x 48½in	2

2. Place the template on one of the dark "geese sky" rectangles – 12¾ x 16¾in for the king or 6¾ x 8¾in for the throw. Trace around the template and cut it out. Repeat with the remaining dark and light rectangles measuring 12¾ x 16¾in or 6¾ x 8¾in, to create four light and four dark right-angle triangles. Set the triangles aside.

4. Using a rotary cutter and ruler, slice the paper template along the dotted line at the bottom as shown (Diagram 1). Using an iron, press one of the dark "flying geese" rectangles – 12¾ x 32¾in for the king, or 6¾ x 16¾in for the throw – in half widthways, and place the modified template on top, with the sliced edge of the template aligned with the folded edge of the fabric as shown (Diagram 2). Trace the template onto the fabric. Leave the fabric folded in half while you cut out the template shape. Open and press to finish one isosceles triangle (Diagram 3). Repeat to make a second isosceles triangle with the remaining dark rectangle measuring 12¾ x 32¾in, or 6¾ x 16¾in.

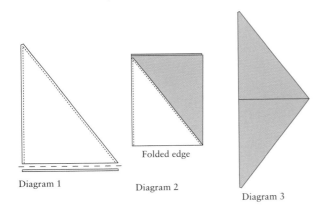

Diagram 1

Folded edge

Diagram 2

Diagram 3

5. Using a rotary cutter, slice the paper template once more, this time along the dotted line on the left side as shown (Diagram 4). Press the light "diamond" rectangle – 24¾ x 32¾in for the king, or 12¾ x 16¾in for the throw – in half lengthways, then press it in half again widthways, and place the modified template on top, with the sliced edges aligned with the folded edges as shown (Diagram 5). Trace the template onto the fabric. Leave the fabric folded while you cut out the template shape. Open and press to finish the light diamond piece (Diagram 6).

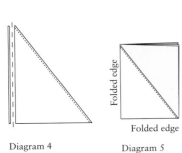

Diagram 4

Folded edge

Folded edge

Diagram 5

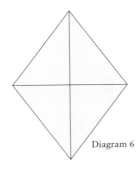

Diagram 6

6. Align one light right-angle triangle to the top right of one of the dark isosceles triangles and stitch it in place as shown (Diagram 7). Press the seam open. Align a second light right-angle triangle to the top left of the dark isosceles triangle and stitch it in place as shown (Diagram 8). Open and press to finish one flying geese unit (Diagram 9). If needed, trim to 12½ x 32½in for the king, or 6½ x 16½in for the throw. Repeat to make a second flying geese unit.

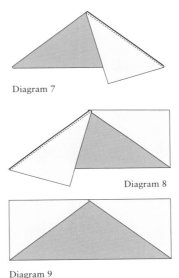

Diagram 7

Diagram 8

Diagram 9

7. Align one dark right-angle triangle to the top left of the light diamond piece, and pin in place. Align another dark right-angle triangle to the bottom right of the light diamond piece, and pin in place. Sew the right-angle triangles to the diamond piece (Diagram 10). Press the seams open.

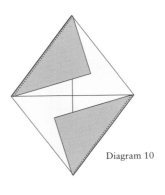

Diagram 10

8. Align one dark right-angle triangle to the top right of the light diamond piece, and pin in place. Align another dark right-angle triangle to the bottom left of the light diamond piece, and pin in place. Sew the right-angle triangles to the diamond piece (Diagram 11). Press the seams open to finish the diamond block (Diagram 12). If needed, trim to 24½ x 32½in for the king, or 12½ x 16½in for the throw.

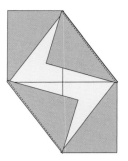

Diagram 11

Diagram 12

ASSEMBLE THE QUILT TOP

9. To make the middle section, sew together the diamond block, the two flying geese units, and the two dark A and two light B rectangles, as shown (Diagram 13), and press the seams open.

Diagram 13

10. To make the top section, sew together two dark C strips, one light D strip, two dark E strips, one light F strip and one light G strip, as shown (Diagram 14), and press the seams open. Repeat with the remaining strips to make the bottom section.

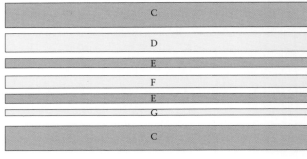

Diagram 14

11. Sew the three sections together as shown (Diagram 15). Press the seams open to finish the quilt top.

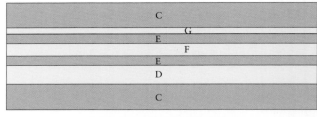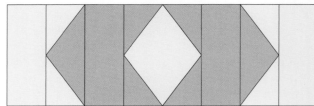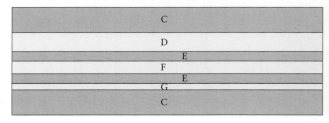

Diagram 15

ASSEMBLING THE QUILT

Refer to pages 36–51 for assembling, quilting and binding your quilt. Turn to page 102 for the assembly diagram and quilting guide.

QUILTING SUGGESTIONS

To finish your quilt like the one pictured, mark your quilting lines as follows:

▶ Begin by marking anchoring lines 2in (5cm) inside and 2in (5cm) around the centre diamond.

▶ Continue marking parallel lines to the diamond in 2–4in (5–10cm) intervals throughout the quilt, allowing the lines to intersect at the edges.

CENTRO

I love working from a coffee shop every so often, and this design was inspired by the seating area in one of my favourites. Coffee shops are meeting points for friends, as well as places for work, creativity and conversations of all kinds. To me, they represent the merging of minds and the human connection that makes living and working as a creative person so special. This quilt allows you to use several different fabrics in one design, so have fun choosing a mix of colours, patterns and textures that play off each other.

SIZE	IMPERIAL	METRIC
Wall hanging	26 x 36in	66 x 91cm

MATERIALS

The default instructions are written for standard fabric with a width of 42in or 107cm.

▶ Fabric 1: Brussels Washer Yarn-Dyed Redrock
▶ Fabric 2: Essex Peach
▶ Fabric 3: Essex Leather
▶ Fabric 4: Essex Ivory wide
▶ Backing: Essex Peach
▶ Binding: Essex Ivory wide
▶ Batting: Quilters Dream Wool

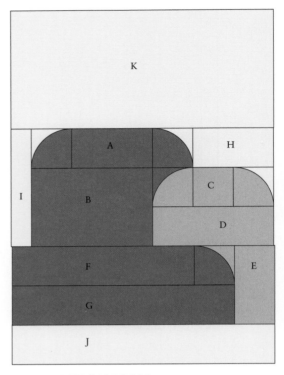

ASSEMBLY DIAGRAM

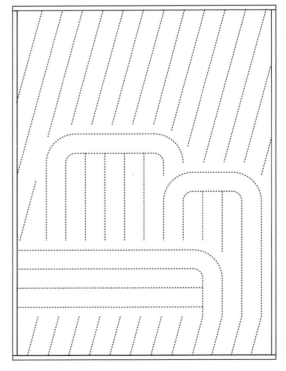

QUILTING GUIDE

WALL HANGING

Fabric	Imperial Standard (42in) or Wide (54in)	Metric Standard (107cm) or Wide (137cm)
Fabric 1 (left arch)	⅓yd	30cm
Fabric 2 (right arch)	¼yd	25cm
Fabric 3 (bottom arch)	⅓yd	30cm
Fabric 4 (background)	⅔yd	60cm
Backing	1yd	95cm
Batting	28 x 38in	71 x 96cm
Binding	⅜yd	35cm

CUTTING INSTRUCTIONS

From Fabric 1 (Rust), cut:
▶ 1 strip 8½in x WOF. Subcut:
  ▶ 1 rectangle 8½ x 12½in (B)
  ▶ 1 rectangle 8½ x 4½in (A)
  ▶ 1 square 4¾ x 4¾in (Concave 1)
  ▶ 2 squares 4½ x 4½in (Convex 1)

From Fabric 2 (Peach), cut:
▶ 1 strip 4¾in x WOF. Subcut:
  ▶ 1 square 4¾ x 4¾in (Concave 2)
  ▶ 1 rectangle 4½ x 12½in (D)
  ▶ 1 rectangle 4½ x 8½in (E)
  ▶ 3 squares 4½ x 4½in
  (Convex 2 and C)

From Fabric 3 (Brown), cut:
▶ 2 strips 4½in x WOF. Subcut:
  ▶ 1 rectangle 4½ x 22½in (G)
  ▶ 1 rectangle 4½ x 18½in (F)
  ▶ 1 square 4½ x 4½in (Convex 3)

From Fabric 4 (White), cut:
▶ 1 strip 12½in x WOF. Subcut:
  ▶ 1 rectangle 12½ x 26½in (K)
  ▶ 3 squares 4¾ x 4¾in (Concave 4)
▶ 1 strip 4½in x WOF. Subcut:
  ▶ 1 rectangle 4½ x 26½in (J)
  ▶ 1 rectangle 4½ x 8½in (H)
▶ 1 strip 2½in x WOF. Subcut:
  ▶ 1 rectangle 2½ x 12½in (I)

From the Backing Fabric, cut:
▶ 1 piece 34 x 42in (86 x 107cm)

From the Batting, cut:
▶ 1 piece 28 x 38in (71 x 96cm)

From Binding Fabric cut:
▶ 4 strips 2½in x WOF

SEWING INSTRUCTIONS

PREPARE THE TEMPLATES AND PIECES

1. Print out the templates from riane-elise.com/quilting-by-hand and cut them out.

2. Align the edge of the convex template with the edge of a fabric 1 4½ x 4½in square (convex 1) as shown (Diagram 1). Trace the curve on the fabric. Cut along your marked line and reserve the convex shape. Using an iron, lightly press the curve in half and mark the centre for future reference. Repeat for the remaining convex pieces. For directional fabrics, flip the template so the convex curve is going in the correct direction on the right side of the fabric – fabrics 1 and 2 have one left-oriented convex curve and one right-oriented convex curve, while fabric 3 has one right-oriented convex curve.

3. Align the edge of the concave template with the edge of a fabric 4 4¾ x 4¾in square (concave 4) as shown (Diagram 2). Trace the curve on the fabric. Cut along your marked line and reserve the outer concave shape. Mark the curve centre for future reference. Repeat for the remaining concave pieces. For directional fabrics, flip the template so the concave curve is going in the correct direction on the right side of the fabric – fabric 1 has one left-oriented concave curve, fabric 2 has one right-oriented concave curve and fabric 4 has one left-oriented concave curve and two right-oriented concave curves.

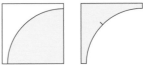

Diagram 2

Diagram 1

SEW THE CURVED PIECES

4. Refer to Sewing Curves on page 33. Using your preferred method, mark, align, pin and sew the convex and concave curves together, following the piecing chart and diagrams to make the correct colour combinations. Press the seams towards the convex pieces.

PIECING CHART

Convex Piece	Concave Piece	Number of pieced squares	Label
Convex 1	Concave 4	2 (one pair of each orientation)	Curve 1
Convex 2	Concave 4	1 (right-oriented)	Curve 2
Convex 2	Concave 1	1 (left-oriented)	Curve 3
Convex 3	Concave 2	1 (right-oriented)	Curve 4

LABELLED CURVES

Curve 1   Curve 2   Curve 3   Curve 4

ASSEMBLE THE QUILT TOP

5. Sew a left-oriented Curve 1 piece to the left side of the A rectangle as shown (Diagram 3). Press the seam open.

Diagram 3

6. Sew the right-oriented Curve 1 piece to the left side of the H rectangle as shown (Diagram 4). Press the seam open.

Diagram 4

7. Sew the Curve 2 and Curve 3 pieces to the right and left sides of the C square as shown (Diagram 5). Press the seams open.

Diagram 5

8. Sew the Curve 4 piece to the right side of the F rectangle as shown (Diagram 6). Press the seam open.

Diagram 6

9. Sew the A unit to the top of the B rectangle as shown (Diagram 7). Press the seam open. Then sew the I rectangle to the left side of the A/B unit and press the seam open.

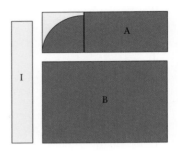

Diagram 7

10. Sew the H unit to the top of the C unit as shown (Diagram 8). Press the seam open. Then sew the D rectangle to the bottom of the H/C unit and press the seam open.

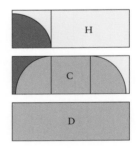

Diagram 8

11. Sew the F unit to the top of the G rectangle and press the seam open. Then sew the E rectangle to the right side of the F/G unit as shown (Diagram 9). Press the seam open.

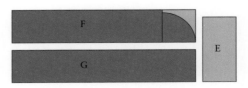

Diagram 9

12. Sew the A/B/I unit to the left side of the H/C/D unit and press the seam open. Sew the F/G/E unit to the bottom of this new unit and press the seam open (Diagram 10).

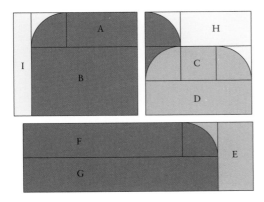

Diagram 10

13. Sew the J and K rectangles to the bottom and top of the quilt (Diagram 11). Press the seams open to finish.

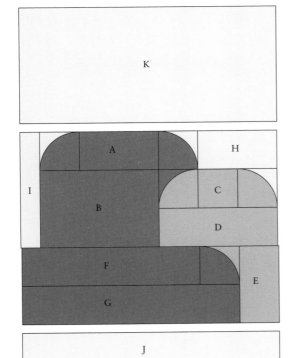

Diagram 11

ASSEMBLING THE QUILT

Refer to pages 36–51 for assembling, quilting and binding your quilt. Turn to page 112 for the assembly diagram and quilting guide.

QUILTING SUGGESTIONS

To finish your quilt like the one pictured, mark your quilting lines as follows:

▶ Inside each curved area, mark one line that echoes the curvature 1in in from the seamline. Then mark an additional echoing line 2in (5cm) in. Fill the inner portion of the blocks with vertical or horizontal lines.

▶ In the background, make 30-degree lines in 2in (5cm) increments.

TIP
Sew small triangles of fabric to the top corners on the backing when attaching the binding. This provides an easy way to hang your quilt!

PORTA

There is a beautiful balance between travelling and being at home. Travel opens my eyes to different ways of living and of being, but it also helps me to appreciate being at home and staying still. This quilt was inspired by the stunning architecture that my sister and I saw on a trip to Lisbon, and it's imbued with all the energy of being on the road and the excitement of soaking up every new experience. Quilting is mostly done at home, quietly by oneself, but I love to bring the spirit of travel into my handwork by reliving memories with every stitch.

SIZE	IMPERIAL	METRIC
Throw	54 x 70in	137 x 178cm
Baby	27 x 35in	69 x 89cm

MATERIALS

The default instructions are written for wide fabric with a width of 54in or 137cm. Variations for standard-width fabric of 42in or 107cm are indicated in the table opposite and given in parentheses in the cutting instructions: Wide (Standard).

▶ Dark Fabric: Essex Yarn-Dyed Lingerie
▶ Light Fabric: Essex Ivory wide
▶ Backing: Essex Yarn-Dyed Lingerie
▶ Binding: Essex Yarn-Dyed Lingerie
▶ Batting: Quilters Dream Wool

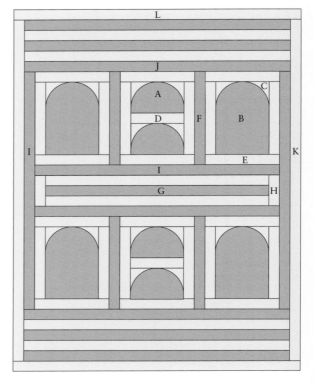

ASSEMBLY DIAGRAM

QUILTING GUIDE

THROW

Fabric	Imperial Standard (42in)	Wide (54in)	Metric Standard (107cm)	Wide (137cm)
Dark	2¾yd	1¾yd	2.55m	1.6m
Light	2⅞yd	2yd	2.65m	1.9m
Backing	3½yd	3½yd	3.15m	3.15m
Batting	56 x 72in	56 x 72in	142 x 183cm	142 x 183cm
Binding	⅝yd	½yd	60cm	50cm

CUTTING INSTRUCTIONS

From the Dark Fabric, cut:
▶ 2 (3) strips 10½in x WOF. Subcut:
  ▶ 4 rectangles 10½ x 14½in (B)
  ▶ 4 rectangles 10½ x 6½in (A)
▶ 13 (22) strips 2½in x WOF. Subcut:
  ▶ 6 strips 2½ x 50½in (J)
  (12 strips 2½ x 25½in)
  ▶ 4 strips 2½ x 46½in (I)
  (8 strips 2½ x 23½in)
  ▶ 1 strip 2½ x 42½in (G)
  (2 strips 2½ x 21½in)
  ▶ 4 strips 2½ x 18½in (F)

From the Light Fabric, cut:
▶ 2 (3) strips 5¾in x WOF. Subcut:
  ▶ 8 rectangles 5¾ x 11in (C)
▶ 20 (30) strips 2½in x WOF. Subcut:
  ▶ 4 strips 2½ x 50½in (J)
  (8 strips 2½ x 25½in)
  ▶ 2 strips 2½ x 42½in (G)
  (4 strips 2½ x 21½in)
  ▶ 4 strips 2½ x 33½in (K)
  ▶ 4 strips 2½ x 27½in (L)
  ▶ 24 strips 2½ x 14½in (E)
  ▶ 2 strips 2½ x 10½in (D)
  ▶ 2 strips 2½ x 6½in (H)

From the Backing Fabric, cut:
▶ 2 pieces 63in x WOF

From the Batting, cut:
▶ 1 piece 56 x 72in (142 x 183cm)

From the Binding Fabric, cut:
▶ 5 (7) strips 2½in x WOF

BABY

Fabric	Imperial		Metric	
	Standard (42in)	Wide (54in)	Standard (107cm)	Wide (137cm)
Dark	⅞yd	½yd	80cm	50cm
Light	¾yd	⅝yd	70cm	60cm
Backing	1¼yd	1yd	1.15m	95cm
Batting	29 x 37in	29 x 37in	74 x 94cm	74 x 94cm
Binding	⅜yd	⅜yd	35cm	35cm

CUTTING INSTRUCTIONS

From the Dark Fabric, cut:
▶ 1 (2) strip(s) 5½in x WOF. Subcut:
  ▸ 4 rectangles 5½ x 7½in (B)
  ▸ 4 rectangles 5½ x 3½in (A)
▶ 7 (11) strips 1½in x WOF. Subcut:
  ▸ 6 strips 1½ x 25½in (J)
  ▸ 4 strips 1½ x 23½in (I)
  ▸ 1 strip 1½ x 21½in (G)
  ▸ 4 strips 1½ x 9½in (F)

From the Light Fabric, cut:
▶ 1 (2) strips 3¼in x WOF. Subcut:
  ▸ 8 rectangles 3¼in x 6in (C)
▶ 10 (12) strips 1½in x WOF. Subcut:
  ▸ 2 strips 1½ x 33½in (K)
  ▸ 2 strips 1½ x 27½in (L)
  ▸ 4 strips 1½ x 25½in (J)
  ▸ 2 strips 1½ x 21½in (G)
  ▸ 24 strips 1½ x 7½in (E)
  ▸ 2 strips 1½ x 5½in (D)
  ▸ 2 strips 1½ x 3½in (H)

From the Backing Fabric, cut:
▶ 1 piece 35 x 43in

From the Batting, cut:
▶ 1 piece 29 x 37in (74 x 94cm)

From the Binding Fabric, cut:
▶ 3 (4) strips 2½in x WOF

SEWING INSTRUCTIONS

ASSEMBLE THE STRIPS (THROW SIZE ONLY)
Depending on the width of fabric you cut from (wide or standard), pair up two of the following strips and sew them together, end to end, to form strips of the appropriate strip size. Skip this step if you are making the baby size.

	Pieced strip size	Number of pieced strip(s)
G strip (dark)*	2½ x 42½in	1
G strip (light)*	2½ x 42½in	2
I strips*	2½ x 46½in	4
J strips (dark)*	2½ x 50½in	6
J strips (light)*	2½ x 50½in	4
K strips	2½ x 66½in	2
L strips	2½ x 54½in	2

Standard-width fabric only

PREPARE CURVED PIECES (THROW & BABY)

1. Print out the templates from <u>riane-elise.com/quilting-by-hand</u> and cut them out.

2. Using an iron, press the dark A and light C rectangles in half widthways, with right sides together as shown (Diagram 1). Press the dark B pieces in half lengthways, forming narrower rectangles (Diagram 1). Leave the pieces folded in half for the next step.

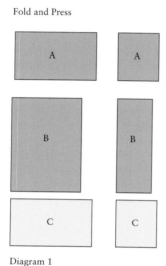

Fold and Press

Diagram 1

3. Align the edge of the convex template with the folded edge and the top of the dark A fabric as shown (Diagram 2). Trace the curve on the fabric and mark the centre line and the bottom edge of the template for future reference. Cut along your marked line and reserve the curved shape (Diagram 3). Repeat to make a total of four convex A pieces.

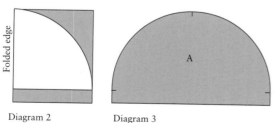

Diagram 2   Diagram 3

4. Align the edge of the convex template with the folded edge of the dark B fabric at the top as shown (Diagram 4). Trace the curve on the fabric and mark the centre line and the bottom edge of the template for future reference. Cut along your marked line and reserve the curved shape (Diagram 5). Repeat to make a total of four convex B pieces.

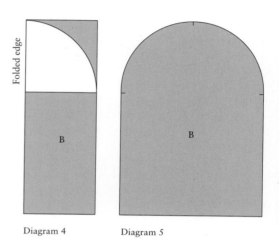

Diagram 4   Diagram 5

5. Align the edge of the concave template with the folded edge of the light C fabric as shown (Diagram 6). Trace the curve on the fabric with a pencil. Cut along your marked line and reserve the outer shape. Mark the centre line for future reference (Diagram 7). Repeat to make a total of eight concave C pieces.

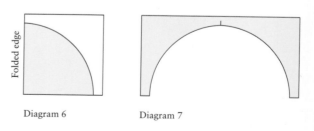

Diagram 6   Diagram 7

TIP

To ensure a clean cut, use a few pins on either side of your marked line to hold the folded layers together.

SEW THE CURVED PIECES

6. Refer to Sewing Curves on page 33. Using your preferred method, mark, align, pin and sew the convex and concave curves together, making a total of four A pieces and four B pieces. Press the seams towards the concave (light) fabric. Line up the bottom edges of the light pieces with the marks you made on the dark pieces to indicate the bottom edge of the convex template (Diagram 8).

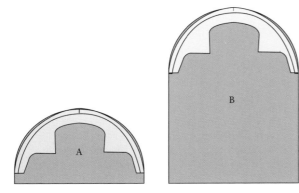

Diagram 8

7. Trim the A pieces to 10½ x 6½in for the throw, or 5½ x 3½in for the baby, making sure to leave ¼in on the sides and top of the curve (Diagram 9).

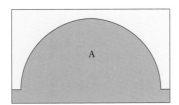

Diagram 9

8. Trim the B pieces to 10½ x 14½in for the throw, or 5½ x 7½in for the baby, making sure to leave ¼in on the top and sides of the curve (Diagram 10).

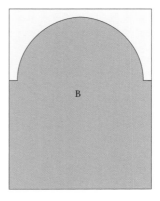

Diagram 10

ASSEMBLE THE ROWS

9. Sew two A pieces together with a D strip between them, and press the seams open (Diagram 11). Sew one E strip to the left side of the A pieces and another to the right side. Press the seams open. Then sew an E strip to the top of the A piece and another to the bottom, pressing the seams open. Repeat to make a second A unit.

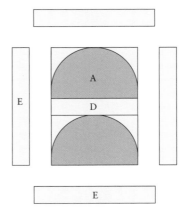

Diagram 11

10. Sew one E strip to the left side of a B piece and another to the right side. Press the seams open. Then sew an E strip to the top of the same B piece and another to the bottom, pressing the seams open (Diagram 12). Repeat with the three remaining B pieces to make a total of four B units.

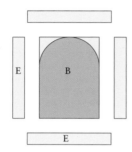

Diagram 12

11. Sew together two B units, one A unit and two F strips as shown (Diagram 13). Press all the seams open to finish Row 1. Repeat with the remaining B, A and F units to make a second Row 1 unit.

Row 1 (Make 2)

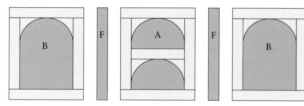

Diagram 13

12. Sew two light G strips together with one dark G strip in between as shown (Diagram 14). Press the seams open. Sew an H rectangle to either end, as shown, pressing the seams open. Sew one I strip to the top of the unit and another to the bottom, and press the seams open to finish Row 2.

Row 2 (Make 1)

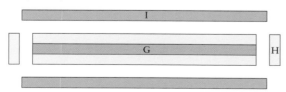

Diagram 14

13. Sew two light J strips and three dark J strips together as shown (Diagram 15). Press the seams open to finish Row 3. Repeat with the remaining J strips to create a second Row 3 unit.

Row 3 (Make 2)

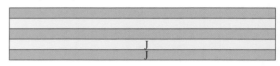

Diagram 15

ASSEMBLE THE QUILT TOP

14. Sew Rows 1 and Row 2 together as shown (Diagram 16), and press the seams open.

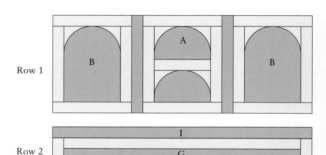

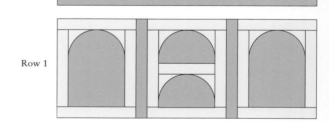

Diagram 16

15. Sew a dark I strip to the left and right sides of the quilt top (Diagram 17). Press the seams open. Then sew one Row 3 unit to the top of the quilt top and the other to the bottom, pressing the seams open.

16. Finish by adding the outer borders. Sew the two K borders to the left and right sides of the quilt top, and press the seams open (Diagram 18). Sew the two L borders to the top and bottom of the quilt top, and press seams open to finish.

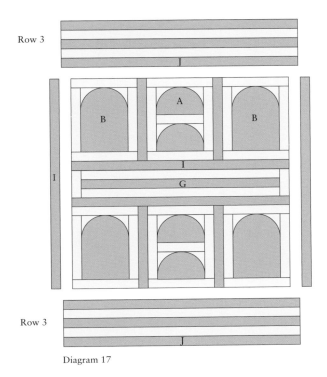

Diagram 17

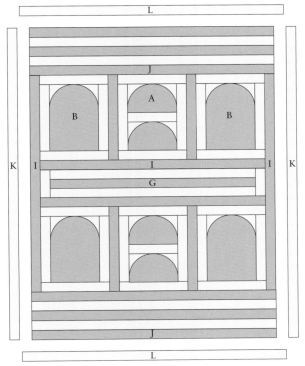

Diagram 18

ASSEMBLING THE QUILT

Refer to pages 36–51 for assembling, quilting and binding your quilt. Turn to page 120 for the assembly diagram and quilting guide.

QUILTING SUGGESTIONS

To finish your quilt like the one pictured, mark your quilting lines as follows:

▶ Use the 30-degree/60-degree line on a quilting ruler to mark intersecting diagonal lines 3in (8cm) apart across the quilt top.

LUNE

This is a quilt for the night owls, the stargazers and those who feel most alive after dark. I have always liked the night-time, and am often more creative, more productive and happier after the sun goes down. No matter where I am in the world, the moon is a constant friend. The half-moon shapes in this quilt are perfect for piecing by hand, perhaps on a cosy evening curled up by the fire.

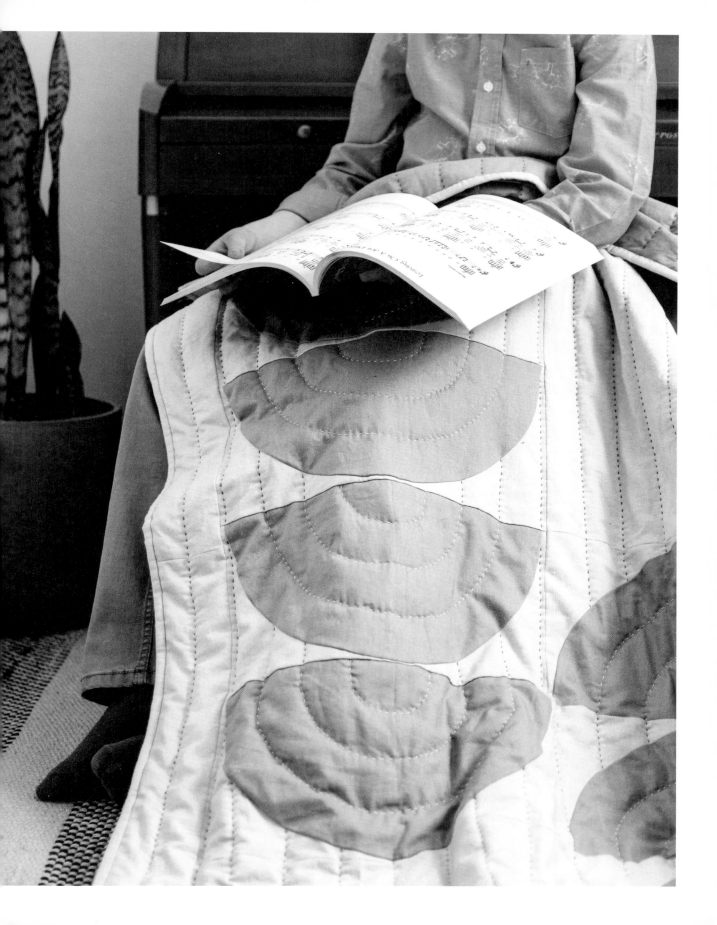

SIZE	IMPERIAL	METRIC
Throw	52 x 56in	132 x 142cm

MATERIALS

The default instructions are written for standard fabric with a width of 42in or 107cm. Variations for wide fabric with a width of 54in or 137cm are indicated in the table opposite and given in parentheses in the cutting instructions: Standard (Wide).

▶ Light Fabric: Essex Putty
▶ Dark Fabric: Essex Natural wide
▶ Backing: Essex Putty
▶ Binding: Essex Natural wide
▶ Batting: Quilters Dream Wool

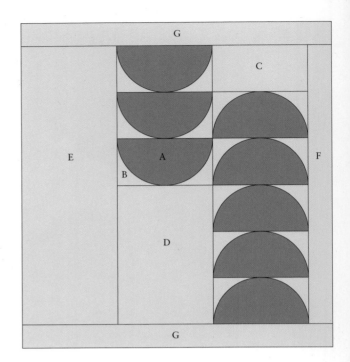

ASSEMBLY DIAGRAM

QUILTING GUIDE

THROW

Fabric	Imperial Standard (42in)	Wide (54in)	Metric Standard (107cm)	Wide (137cm)
Dark	1⅛yd	⅞yd	1.05m	80cm
Light	3⅜yd	2¼yd	3.1m	2.1m
Backing	3⅓yd	3⅓yd	3.05m	3.05m
Batting	54 x 58in	54 x 58in	137 x 147cm	137 x 147cm
Binding	½yd	½yd	50cm	50cm

CUTTING INSTRUCTIONS

From the Dark Fabric, cut:
▶ 4 (3) strips 8½in x WOF. Subcut:
  ▶ 8 rectangles 8½ x 16½in (A)

From the Light Fabric, cut:
▶ 3 (2) strips 16½in x WOF. Subcut:
  ▶ 2 rectangles 16½ x 24½in (E)
  (1 strip 16 x 48½in)
  ▶ 1 rectangle 16½ x 24½in (D)
  ▶ 1 rectangle 16½ x 8½in (C)
▶ 4 (3) strips 8¾in x WOF. Subcut:
  ▶ 8 rectangles 8¾ x 17in (B)
▶ 6 (3) strips 4½in x WOF. Subcut:
  ▶ 4 rectangles 4½ x 26½in (G)
  (2 strips 4½ x 52½in)
  ▶ 2 rectangles 4½ x 24½in (F)
  (1 strip 4½ x 48½in)

From the Backing Fabric, cut:
▶ 2 pieces 60in x WOF

From the Batting, cut:
▶ 1 piece 54 x 58in (137 x 147cm)

From the Binding Fabric, cut:
▶ 6 (5) strips 2½in x WOF

SEWING INSTRUCTIONS

PREPARE THE TEMPLATES AND PIECES

1. Print out the concave and convex templates from riane-elise.com/quilting-by-hand and cut them out.

2. If you are using standard-width fabric for the light pieces, sew two of the following letter strips together, end to end, to form strips of the appropriate strip size, and press seams open. If you are using wide fabric for the light pieces, skip this step.

	Strip size	Number of pieced strip(s)
E strip	16½ x 48½in	1
F strip	4½ x 48½in	1
G strips	4½ x 52½in	2

3. Using an iron, press the dark A rectangles in half widthways. Likewise, press the light B rectangles in half widthways (Diagram 1). Leave them folded for the next step.

Fold and Press

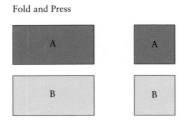

Diagram 1

4. Align the edge of the convex template with the folded edge of the folded A rectangle as shown (Diagram 2). Trace the curve on the fabric. Cut along your marked line and reserve the curved shape. Mark the centre top for future reference (Diagram 3). Repeat to make eight half-circle A pieces.

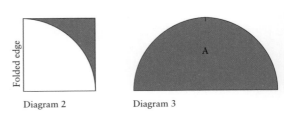

Diagram 2   Diagram 3

5. Align the edge of the concave template with the folded edge of the folded B rectangles as shown (Diagram 4). Trace the curve on the fabric. Cut along your marked line and reserve the outer shape. Mark the centre top for future reference (Diagram 5). Repeat to make eight concave B pieces.

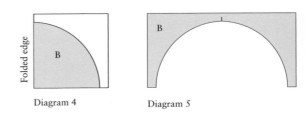

Diagram 4   Diagram 5

TIP
To ensure a nice, clean cut, use a few pins on either side of the marked line to hold the folded layers together.

SEW THE CURVED PIECES

6. Refer to Sewing Curves on page 33. Using your preferred method, mark, align, pin and sew the convex and concave curves together, making a total of eight half-circle rectangles. Press the seams towards the concave (light) fabric.

7. Trim the half-circle rectangles to 8½ x 16½in, making sure to leave ¼in on the sides and top of the curve (Diagram 6).

Diagram 6

ASSEMBLE THE QUILT TOP

8. Sew three half-circle rectangles together with the D rectangle to form one column, and sew five half-circle rectangles together with the C rectangle to form a second column, as shown (Diagram 7). Press the seams away from the curves (towards the light fabric). Place right sides of the fabric together and bring the seams in line so they "nest" neatly together. Pin in place and sew the two columns together down the centre and press the seam open.

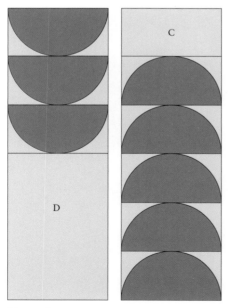

Diagram 7

9. Sew the E strip to the left side of your quilt top and press the seam away from the curves. Sew the F strip to the right side of your quilt top and press the seam away from the curves (Diagram 8).

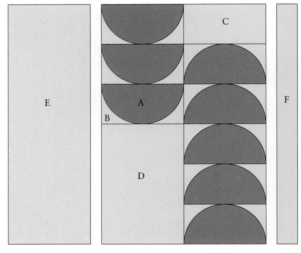

Diagram 8

10. Finish the quilt top by adding the G borders to the top and bottom of the quilt top. Press the seams away from the curves to finish (Diagram 9).

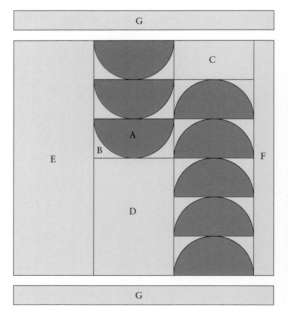

Diagram 9

ASSEMBLING THE QUILT

Refer to pages 36–51 for assembling, quilting and binding your quilt. Turn to page 130 for the assembly diagram and quilting guide.

QUILTING SUGGESTIONS

To finish your quilt like the one pictured, mark your quilting lines as follows:

▶ Within each half-circle, mark three curved lines 2in (5cm) from the edge and in 2in (5cm) increments from each other.

▶ On the background fabric, mark vertical lines in 2in (5cm) increments.

PANTO

This sweet pattern reminds me of gentle hills or rolling waves, depending on the scenery I'm craving most. The design is perfect for hand-piecing both straight and curved seams in one quilt. As it's composed of relatively few pieces, Panto comes together quickly and easily. Mimic the flow of the curves in your quilting for an extra-special finish.

SIZE	IMPERIAL	METRIC
Throw	60 x 58in	152 x 147cm

MATERIALS

The default instructions are written for wide fabric with a width of 54in or 137cm. Due to the size of this project, there is no difference in the instructions or materials needed if using standard-width fabric.

▶ Dark Fabric: Brussels Washer O.D. Green
▶ Light Fabric: Essex Natural wide
▶ Backing: Brussels Washer O.D. Green
▶ Binding: Brussels Washer O.D. Green
▶ Batting: Quilters Dream Wool

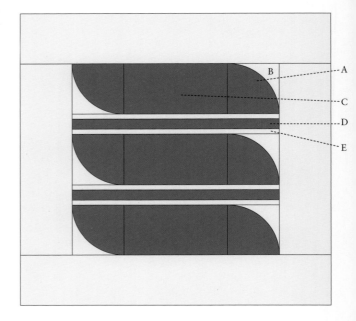

ASSEMBLY DIAGRAM

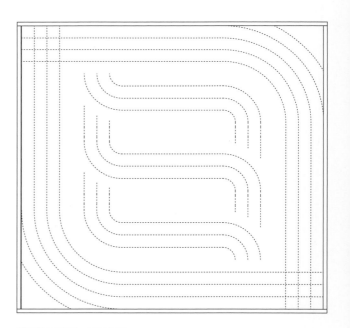

QUILTING GUIDE

THROW

Fabric	Imperial Standard (42in) or Wide (54in)	Metric Standard (107cm) or Wide (137cm)
Dark	1⅛yd	1.05m
Light	2¾yd	2.55m
Backing	3¾yd	3.45m
Batting	62 x 60in	157 x 152cm
Binding	½yd	50cm

CUTTING INSTRUCTIONS

From the Dark Fabric, cut:
▶ 3 strips 10½in x WOF. Subcut:
  ▶ 3 rectangles 10½ x 20½in (C)
  ▶ 6 squares 10½ x 10½in (A)
▶ 2 strips 2½in x WOF. Subcut:
  ▶ 2 strips 2½ x 40½in (D)

From the Light Fabric, cut:
▶ 2 strips 10¾in x WOF. Subcut:
  ▶ 6 squares 10¾ x 10¾in (B)
▶ 6 strips 10½in x WOF. Subcut:
  ▶ 2 rectangles 10½ x 38½in
  ▶ 4 strips 10½ x 30½in
▶ 4 strips 1½in x WOF. Subcut:
  ▶ 4 strips 1½ x 40½in (E)

From the Backing Fabric, cut:
▶ 2 pieces 66in x WOF

From the Batting, cut:
▶ 1 piece 62 x 60in (157 x 152cm)

From the Binding Fabric, cut:
▶ Wide: 5 strips 2½in x WOF
▶ Standard: 6 strips 2½in x WOF

SEWING INSTRUCTIONS

PREPARE THE TEMPLATES AND PIECES

1. Sew two of the light 10½ x 30½in strips together, end to end, to form a top border that measures 10½ x 60½in. Using an iron, press the seam open. Repeat to make a bottom border, and set both borders aside.

2. Print out the templates from riane-elise.com/quilting-by-hand and cut them out.

3. Align the convex template with one of the dark A squares as shown (Diagram 1). Mark the curve and cut it out along the marked line. Lightly press the curve in half and mark the centre. Repeat with the five remaining dark A squares.

Diagram 1

4. Align the concave template with one of the light B squares as shown (Diagram 2). Mark the curve and cut it out along the marked line. Fold the curve in half and mark the centre. Repeat with the five remaining light B squares.

Diagram 2

SEW THE CURVED PIECES

5. Refer to Sewing Curves on page 33. Using your preferred method, mark, align, pin and sew the convex and concave curves together, making a total of six curved squares. Press the seams towards the concave (light) fabric. Trim the curved squares to 10½ x 10½in.

ASSEMBLE THE QUILT TOP

6. Sew one quarter-circle to either end of a C rectangle as shown (Diagram 3). Press the seams open. Repeat twice more with the remaining four quarter-circles and two C rectangles to make a total of three rows.

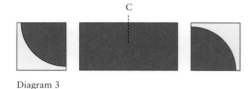

Diagram 3

7. Sew an E strip on either side of a D strip as shown (Diagram 4). Press the seams open. Repeat once more with the remaining two E strips and one D strip to make a second striped row.

Diagram 4

8. Sew the three curved rows from Step 6 together, with the two striped rows from Step 7 in between them, as shown (Diagram 5). Press the seams open.

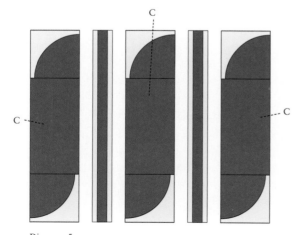

Diagram 5

9. Sew one light 10½ x 38½in rectangle to the left side of the quilt top and the other to the right, as shown (Diagram 6). Press the seams open.

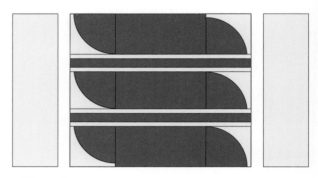

Diagram 6

10. Sew the two 10½ x 60½in borders from Step 1 to the top and bottom of the quilt top as shown (Diagram 7). Press the seams open to finish the quilt top.

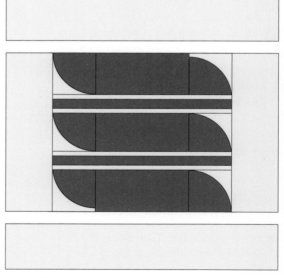

Diagram 7

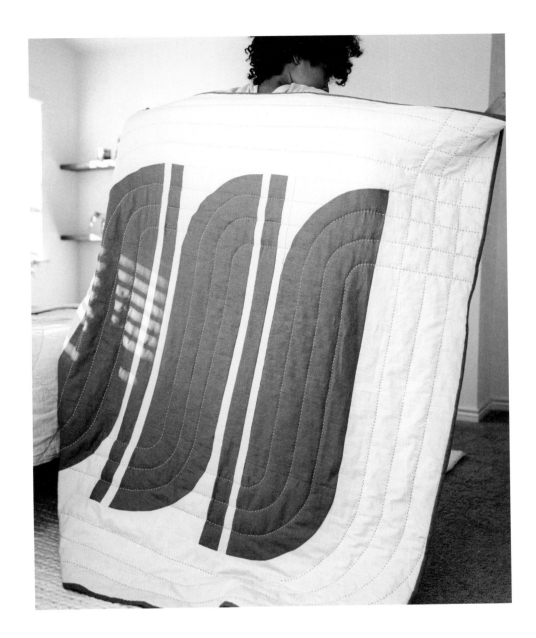

ASSEMBLING THE QUILT

Refer to pages 36–51 for assembling, quilting and binding your quilt. Turn to page 138 for the assembly diagram and quilting guide.

QUILTING SUGGESTIONS

To finish your quilt like the one pictured, mark your quilting lines as follows:

▶ For each of the curved pieces, mark three lines at 2½in (7cm) increments inside from the inside edge of the curve. Draw a straight line through the centre of the dark section to connect the lines. Extend the lines down through the background fabric to the top and bottom of the quilt. Extend the lines from the middle curved section to the upper and lower curved sections.

▶ In the upper right and lower left corners of the quilt, echo the curved piecing with five curved lines 2½in (7cm) apart. Extend these lines to the lower right and upper left corners of the quilt, intersecting them in these corners.

CURIO

Patchwork, the traditional method of piecing together small squares of fabric, has become almost synonymous with quilting and is often a new quilter's introduction to quilt-making. Curio is an ode to patchwork in all its beautiful forms. I love it in these modern, muted tones, but for the next version I make, I plan on upending my scrap bin and including a bit of all my favourite fabrics. The traditional hand tying on this quilt is also a nod to the customs of past generations, and I love how the ties add texture and a touch of whimsy. For some reason, this quilt is the one I keep in my car to use for picnicking with friends or family.

SIZE	IMPERIAL	METRIC
Throw	57½ x 52½in	146 x 133cm

This pattern can easily be scaled up or down to suit your needs. To learn more about scaling, please see Scaling Patterns on page 24.

SCALING SUGGESTIONS

▶ *King:* Scale up by 200 per cent to make a quilt that finishes at 115 x 105in or 292 x 267cm
▶ *Baby:* Scale down by 50 per cent to make a quilt that finishes at 28¾ x 26¼in or 73 x 67cm

MATERIALS

The default instructions are written for wide fabric with a width of 54in or 137cm. Variations for standard-width fabric of 42in or 107cm are indicated in the table opposite and given in parentheses in the cutting instructions: Wide (Standard).

▶ Dark Fabric: Essex Natural wide
▶ Light Fabric: Essex Ivory wide
▶ Backing: Essex Ivory wide
▶ Binding: Essex Ivory wide
▶ Batting: Quilters Dream Wool

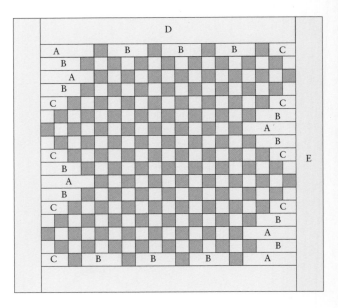

ASSEMBLY DIAGRAM

QUILTING GUIDE

THROW

Fabric	Imperial Standard (42in)	Wide (54in)	Metric Standard (107cm)	Wide (137cm)
Dark	1yd	¾yd	95cm	70cm
Light	2⅝yd	2yd	2.4m	1.85m
Backing	3⅜yd	3⅜yd	3.1m	3.1m
Batting	59½ x 54½in	59½ x 54½in	151 x 138cm	151 x 138cm
Binding	½yd	½yd	50cm	50cm

CUTTING INSTRUCTIONS

From the Dark Fabric, cut:
▶ 8 (10) strips 3in x WOF. Subcut:
  ▶ 128 squares 3 x 3in

From the Light Fabric, cut:
▶ 4 (8) strips 5½in x WOF. Subcut:
  ▶ 2 strips 5½ x 53in (E)
  (4 strips 5½ x 26¾in)
  ▶ 2 strips 5½ x 48in (D)
  (4 strips 5½ x 24¼in)
▶ 12 (14) strips 3in x WOF. Subcut:
  ▶ 6 rectangles 3 x 10½in (A)
  ▶ 14 rectangles 3 x 8in (B)
  ▶ 8 rectangles 3 x 5½in (C)
  ▶ 113 squares 3 x 3in

From the Backing Fabric, cut:
▶ 2 pieces 60½in x WOF

From the Batting, cut:
▶ 1 piece 59½ x 54½in (151 x 138cm)

From the Binding Fabric cut:
▶ 5 (6) strips 2½in x WOF

Follow this visual for quick reference on how many pieces you'll need to cut for each size.

Piece count:

▩	128
☐	113
A	6
B	14
C	8

SEWING INSTRUCTIONS

ASSEMBLE THE STRIPS

1. Sew one A rectangle, eight dark 3 x 3in squares and seven light 3 x 3in squares together, as shown, to form an A strip (Diagram 1). Press all the seams open. Repeat to make a total of four A strips.

Diagram 1   A Strip (Make 4)

2. Sew one B rectangle, eight dark 3 x 3in squares and eight light 3 x 3in squares together, as shown, to form a B strip (Diagram 2). Press all the seams open. Repeat to make a total of eight B strips.

Diagram 2   B Strip (Make 8)

3. Sew two C rectangles, eight dark 3 x 3in squares and seven light 3 x 3in squares together, as shown, to form a C strip (Diagram 3). Press all the seams open. Repeat to make a total of three C strips.

Diagram 3   C Strip (Make 3)

4. Sew one A rectangle, three B rectangles, one C rectangle and four dark 3 x 3in squares together, as shown, to form an A/B/C strip (Diagram 4). Press all the seams open. Repeat to make a total of two A/B/C strips.

Diagram 4   A/B/C Strip (Make 2)

ASSEMBLE THE QUILT TOP

5. Following the Assembly Diagram on page 144, sew the strips together in the orientation shown to assemble the centre of the quilt top. Press all the seams open.

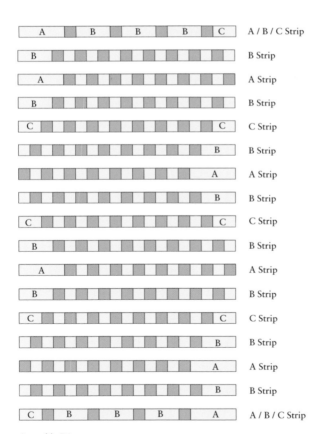

Assembly Diagram

6. If you are using standard-width fabric, sew two D strips together, end to end, to form a D border. Press the seams open and repeat to make a second D border. Then sew two E strips together, end to end, to form an E border. Press the seams open and repeat to make a second E border. Skip this step if you are using wide fabric.

7. Sew a D border to the top and bottom of the quilt top and press the seams open (Diagram 5).

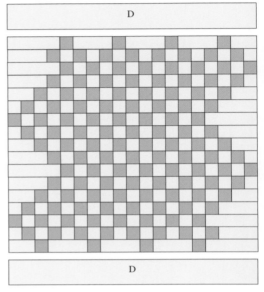

Diagram 5

8. Sew an E border to the left and right sides of the quilt top and press the seams open (Diagram 6).

Diagram 6

ASSEMBLING THE QUILT

Refer to pages 36–51 for assembling, quilting and binding your quilt. Turn to page 144 for the assembly diagram and quilting guide.

QUILTING SUGGESTIONS

To finish your quilt like the one pictured, mark your tying points as follows:

▶ In the middle of each light square, mark a small dot. Mark dots with similar spacing in the background and borders.

UNION

This design reminds me of people coming together, supporting each other and holding dear ones close. The design looks simple, but the thin strips and some bias edges make Union one of the more technical quilts in this book. A little practice goes a long way, however, and it's satisfying when quilts challenge us to improve our skills, even in seemingly small ways such as trying to achieve consistent seam allowances. Go easy on yourself if this quilt takes time (and maybe phone a friend when you need a break).

SIZE	IMPERIAL	METRIC
Throw	50 x 50in	127 x 127cm

MATERIALS

The default instructions are written for standard fabric with a width of 42in or 107cm. Variations for wide fabric with a width of 54in or 137cm are indicated in the table opposite and given in parentheses in the cutting instructions: Standard (Wide).

▶ Dark Fabric: Essex Ochre YD
▶ Light Fabric: Essex Ivory wide
▶ Backing: Brussels Washer Yarn-Dyed Redrock
▶ Binding: Essex Ochre YD
▶ Batting: Quilters Dream Wool

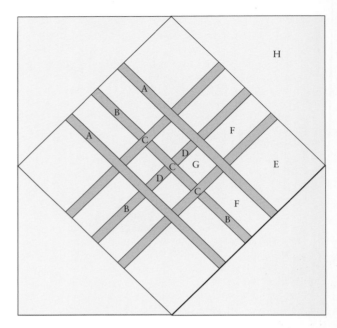

ASSEMBLY DIAGRAM

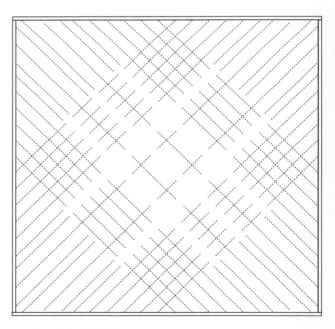

QUILTING GUIDE

THROW

Fabric	Imperial Standard (42in)	Wide (54in)	Metric Standard (107cm)	Wide (137cm)
Dark	⅜yd	⅓yd	35cm	30cm
Light	3yd	1⅝yd	2.75m	1.5m
Backing	3¼yd	1½yd	3m	1.4m
Batting	52 x 52in	52 x 52in	132 x 132cm	132 x 132cm
Binding	½yd	⅜yd	50cm	35cm

CUTTING INSTRUCTIONS

From the Dark Fabric, cut:
▶ 6 (5) strips 2in x WOF. Subcut:
  ▶ 2 strips 2 x 36in (A)
  ▶ 8 rectangles 2 x 11½in (B)
  ▶ 3 rectangles 2 x 11in (C)
  ▶ 2 rectangles 2 x 5in (D)

From the Light Fabric, cut:
▶ 2 (1) strip(s) 26in x WOF. Subcut:
  ▶ 2 squares 26 x 26in (H)
▶ 2 (1) strip(s) 11½in x WOF. Subcut:
  ▶ 4 squares 11½ x 11½in (E)
▶ 4 (3) strips 5in x WOF. Subcut:
  ▶ 8 rectangles 5 x 11½in (F)
  ▶ 4 squares 5 x 5in (G)

From the Backing Fabric, cut:
▶ *Standard:* 2 pieces 58in x WOF
▶ *Wide:* 1 piece 54in x WOF

From the Batting, cut:
▶ 1 piece 52 x 52in (132 x 132cm)

From the Binding Fabric, cut:
▶ 6 (4) strips 2½in x WOF

SEWING INSTRUCTIONS

ASSEMBLE THE QUILT TOP

1. Sew two light G squares to a dark D rectangle as shown (Diagram 1). Press the seams open. Repeat to make a second G/D unit.

Diagram 1

2. Sew the two G/D units together with a dark C rectangle in between as shown (Diagram 2). Press the seams open.

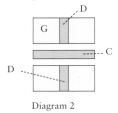

Diagram 2

3. Sew two light F rectangles to a dark B rectangle as shown (Diagram 3). Press the seams open. Repeat to make a second F/B unit.

Diagram 3

4. Sew three dark B rectangles, two light E squares and two light F rectangles together, as shown, to make an upper row (Diagram 4). Press the seams open. Repeat to make a lower row.

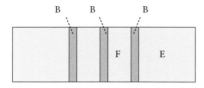

Diagram 4

5. Sew the G/D/C unit, the two F/B units and two dark C rectangles together, as shown, to create the middle row (Diagram 5). Press the seams open.

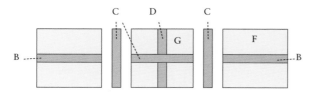

Diagram 5

6. Sew the upper row, middle row and lower rows together, as shown, using the two dark A strips as sashing in between them (Diagram 6). Press the seams open.

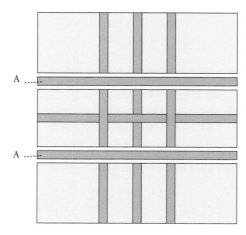

Diagram 6

7. Cut the H squares in half diagonally to make triangles. Align the centre of an H triangle with the centre of one side of the quilt (the centre B strip) and pin in place. Sew the H triangle to the side of the quilt top. Press seams open and repeat with the remaining H triangles (Diagram 7).

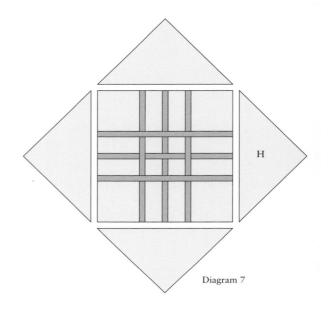

Diagram 7

8. Trim edges as needed and rotate the quilt to finish (Diagram 8).

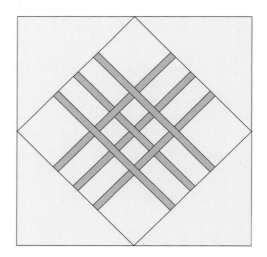

Diagram 8

ASSEMBLING THE QUILT

Refer to pages 36–51 for assembling, quilting and binding your quilt. Turn to page 150 for the assembly diagram and quilting guide.

QUILTING SUGGESTIONS

To finish your quilt like the one pictured, mark your quilting lines as follows:

▶ Use the 45-degree line on a quilting ruler to mark intersecting diagonal lines 3in (8cm) apart across the quilt top.

SYLVAN

Before a season of being grounded and settling into the comfort of home, I enjoyed travelling regularly for work and pleasure. I always loved flying through cascades of pillowy clouds and feeling so small for a moment or two. Sylvan reminds me of peacefully watching the world go by, from 35,000 feet in the air on the way to a new destination. It's a reminder of the freedom and calm that come from seeing things with a new perspective, and I hold this quilt dear whenever my wanderlust surfaces.

SIZE	IMPERIAL	METRIC
Baby	46 x 52in	117 x 132cm

MATERIALS

The default instructions are written for wide fabric with a width of 54in or 137cm. Variations for standard-width fabric of 42in or 107cm are indicated in the table opposite and given in parentheses in the cutting instructions: Wide (Standard).

▶ Dark Fabric: Essex Natural wide
▶ Light Fabric: Essex Ivory wide
▶ Backing: Brussels Washer O.D. Green
▶ Binding: Essex Ivory wide
▶ Batting: Quilters Dream Wool

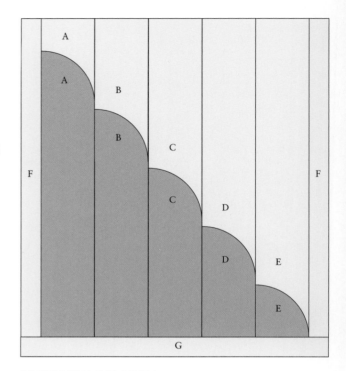

ASSEMBLY DIAGRAM

QUILTING GUIDE

BABY

Fabric	Imperial Standard (42in)	Wide (54in)	Metric Standard (107cm)	Wide (137cm)
Dark	1⅛yd	⅞yd	1.05m	80cm
Light	2yd	1½yd	1.85m	1.4m
Backing	3yd	1⅔yd	2.75m	1.55m
Batting	48 x 54in	48 x 54in	122 x 137cm	122 x 137cm
Binding	½yd	⅜yd	50cm	35cm

CUTTING INSTRUCTIONS

From the Dark Fabric, cut:
▶ 3 (4) strips 8½in x WOF. Subcut:
  ▶ 1 strip 8½ x 44½in (A)
  (2 strips 8½ x 22½in)
  ▶ 1 (1) strip 8½ x 35½in (B)
  ▶ 1 (1) strip 8½ x 26½in (C)
  ▶ 1 (1) rectangle 8½ x 17½in (D)
  ▶ 1 (1) square 8½ x 8½in (E)

From the Light Fabric, cut:
▶ 4 (5) strips 8¾in x WOF. Subcut:
  ▶ 1 strip 8¾ x 49½in (E)
  (2 strips 8¾ x 25in)
  ▶ 1 strip 8¾ x 40½in (D)
  ▶ 1 strip 8¾ x 31½in (C)
  ▶ 1 strip 8¾ x 22½in (B)
  ▶ 1 rectangle 8¾ x 13½in (A)
▶ 3 (6) strips 3½in x WOF. Subcut:
  ▶ 2 strips 3½ x 49½in (F)
  (4 strips 3½ x 25in)
  ▶ 1 strip 3½ x 46½in (G)
  (2 strips 3½ x 23½in)

From the Backing Fabric, cut:
▶ Standard: 2 pieces 60in x WOF
▶ Wide: 1 piece 60in x WOF

From the Batting, cut:
▶ 1 piece 48 x 54in (123 x 137cm)

From the Binding Fabric, cut:
▶ 4 (6) strips 2½in x WOF

SEWING INSTRUCTIONS

PREPARE THE TEMPLATES AND PIECES

1. Print out the templates from riane-elise.com/quilting-by-hand and cut them out.

2. If you are using standard-width fabric, sew two of the following letter strips together, end to end, to form strips of the appropriate size. Press the seams open. If you are using wide fabric, skip this step.

	Pieced strip size	Number of pieced strip(s)
A strips (dark)	8½ x 44½in	1
F strips (light)	3½ x 49½in	2
G strips (light)	3½ x 46½in	1

3. For the light A, B, C, D and E pieces, use the concave template. Starting with the A piece, align the template at the bottom of the strip as shown (Diagram 1). Mark the curve (you do not need to mark the top of the template). Repeat for the light B, C, D and E pieces.

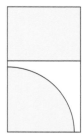

Diagram 1

4. For the dark A, B, C, D and E pieces, use the convex template. For each piece, align the template at the top of the strip as shown (Diagram 2). Mark the curve and make a small mark at the bottom of the template (this will help you line up the convex and concave pieces in Step 6, below). Repeat until all of the dark A, B, C, D and E pieces are marked.

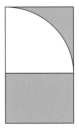

Diagram 2

5. For all the light and dark A, B, C, D and E pieces, cut along the marked curved lines. For the light pieces, reserve the concave piece. For the dark pieces, reserve the convex piece. Lightly press each curve in half and mark the centre (Diagram 3).

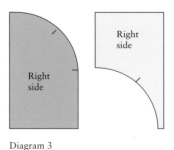

Diagram 3

SEW THE CURVED PIECES

6. Refer to Sewing Curves on page 33. Pair up the corresponding light and dark pieces of the same letter. Using your preferred method, mark, align, pin and sew the convex and concave curves of each pair together. Press all the seams towards the concave (light) sections.

TIP

With right sides together, pin the centre (Diagram 4), then pin the left-side leg of the light curve to the top left corner of the dark curve. Pin the right-side leg of the light A curve to the right side of the dark B curve at the place where you made the mark in Step 4. Add additional pins as desired.

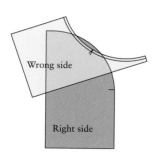

Diagram 4

7. Trim each pieced strip to 8½ x 49½in. The finished columns should look like the pieces shown (Diagram 5).

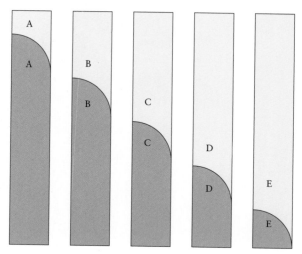

Diagram 5

ASSEMBLE THE QUILT TOP

8. Assemble the quilt top by sewing the columns together as shown (Diagram 6). Press the seams open.

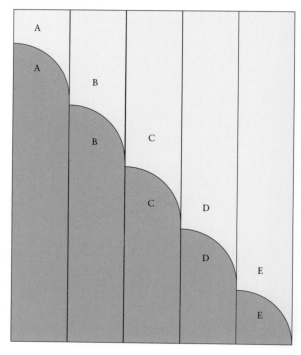

Diagram 6

9. Attach the F borders to the left and right sides of the quilt top, pressing the seams open. Sew the G border to the bottom of the quilt top and press the seam open to finish (Diagram 7).

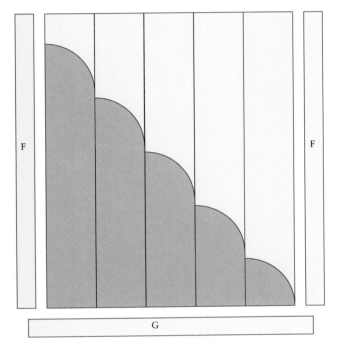

Diagram 7

ASSEMBLING THE QUILT
Refer to pages 36–51 for assembling, quilting and binding your quilt. Turn to page 156 for the assembly diagram and quilting guide.

QUILTING SUGGESTIONS
To finish your quilt like the one pictured, mark your quilting lines as follows:

▶ Use the 45-degree line on a quilting ruler to mark diagonal lines from the bottom left corner of the quilt up to the top right corner.

▶ Mark the lines 2in (5cm) apart across the quilt top.

LIKENESS

Some of the best things in life seem a certain way at first, but then open up to show you a different, more beautiful version. Often, these things take time to fully realize, and this quilt embodies that process and reminds me of that feeling. During each phase of its creation, the Likeness quilt revealed a little more about what it was becoming, and as you piece it I think you'll see what I mean. The blocks themselves are fairly ordinary, but as they come together and as you choose a quilting motif (in your own unique style), you can add new layers of complexity to make this quilt something special.

SIZE	IMPERIAL	METRIC
Throw	48 x 44in	122 x 112cm

MATERIALS

The default instructions are written for standard fabric with a width of 42in or 107cm. Variations for wide fabric with a width of 54in or 137cm are indicated in the table opposite and given in parentheses in the cutting instructions: Standard (Wide).

▶ Dark Fabric: Essex Leather
▶ Light Fabric: Essex Ivory wide
▶ Backing: Brussels Washer O.D. Green
▶ Binding: Brussels Washer O.D. Green
▶ Batting: Quilters Dream Wool

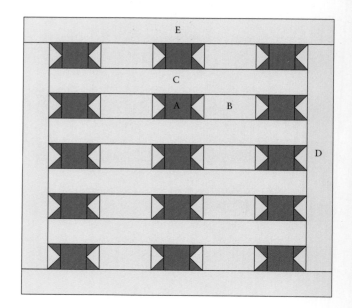

ASSEMBLY DIAGRAM

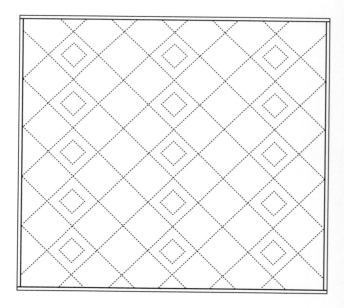

QUILTING GUIDE

THROW

Fabric	Imperial		Metric	
	Standard (42in)	Wide (54in)	Standard (107cm)	Wide (137cm)
Dark	⅝yd	½yd	60cm	50cm
Light	2yd	1½yd	1.85m	1.4m
Backing	3yd	1½yd	2.75m	1.4m
Batting	50 x 46in	50 x 46in	127 x 117cm	127 x 117cm
Binding	½yd	⅜yd	50cm	35cm

CUTTING INSTRUCTIONS

From the Dark Fabric, cut:
▶ 2 (2) strips 4½in x WOF. Subcut:
  ▶ 15 squares 4½ x 4½in (A)
▶ 4 (3) strips 2½in x WOF. Subcut:
  ▶ 60 squares 2½ x 2½in

From the Light Fabric, cut:
▶ 11 (9) strips 4½in x WOF. Subcut:
  ▶ 4 strips 4½ x 40½in (C)
  ▶ 2 strips 4½ x 36½in (D)
  ▶ 4 strips 4½ x 24½in (E)
  (2 strips 4½ x 48½in)
  ▶ 10 rectangles 4½ x 8½in (B)
▶ 4 (3) strips 2½in x WOF. Subcut:
  ▶ 30 rectangles 2½ x 4½in

From the Backing Fabric, cut:
▶ Standard: 2 pieces 54in x WOF
▶ Wide: 1 piece 54in x WOF

From the Batting, cut:
▶ 1 piece 50 x 46in (127 x 117cm)

From the Binding Fabric, cut:
▶ 5 (4) strips 2½in x WOF

SEWING INSTRUCTIONS

PREPARE THE PIECES
1. If you are using standard-width light fabric, sew two 4½ x 24½in E strips together, end to end, to make an E strip measuring 4½ x 48½in. Press the seam open. Repeat to make a second E strip.

ASSEMBLE THE FLYING GEESE
2. Place a dark 2½ x 2½in square on top of a light 2½ x 4½in rectangle, with right sides together and the right-hand edges aligned. Sew from the bottom right corner to the top left corner of the square (Diagram 1). Trim off the top right corner, cutting ¼in away from the seam, and press the seam open.

3. Place a second dark 2½ x 2½in square on top of the same 2½ x 4½in rectangle, this time aligning the left-hand edges. Sew from the bottom left corner to the top right corner of the square (Diagram 2). Trim off the top left corner, cutting ¼in away from the seam, and press the seam open to finish the flying-geese unit. If needed, trim the flying-geese unit to 2½ x 4½in, making sure you leave ¼in above the point of the flying geese.

Diagram 2

4. Repeat Steps 2–3 to make a total of 30 flying-geese units.

Diagram 1

ASSEMBLE THE QUILT TOP

5. Sew two flying-geese units to a dark A square as shown (Diagram 3). Press the seams open. Repeat to make a total of 15 of these A units.

Diagram 3

6. Sew three A units together with two light B rectangles in between them (Diagram 4). Press the seams open. Repeat to make a total of five rows.

Diagram 4

7. Sew the rows together with the four light C strips in between them as shown (Diagram 5). Press the seams open.

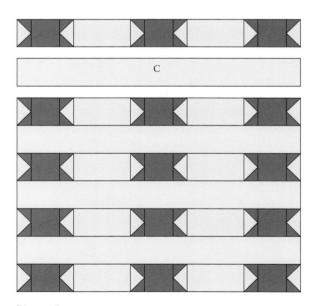

Diagram 5

8. Sew the two light D strips to either side of the quilt top as shown (Diagram 6). Press the seams open.

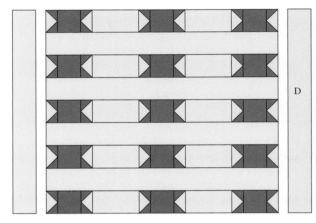

Diagram 6

9. Sew the two E strips to the top and bottom of the quilt top as shown (Diagram 7). Press the seams open to finish.

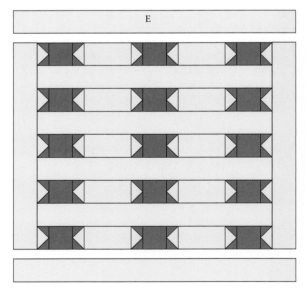

Diagram 7

ASSEMBLING THE QUILT

Refer to pages 36–51 for assembling, quilting and binding your quilt. Turn to page 164 for the assembly diagram and quilting guide.

QUILTING SUGGESTIONS

To finish your quilt like the one pictured, mark your quilting lines as follows:

▶ Mark the centre of each side of the dark 4 x 4in squares, and draw lines to connect them in a diamond shape.

▶ Mark the centre edges of each flying-geese unit, opposite the points. Mark lines connecting these marks to form intersecting 45-degree lines in the background of the quilt.

RITUAL

The block design that makes up this quilt is centuries old and has various names in different parts of the world, but I know it as the Sawtooth Star. I love modifying traditional designs to update them for modern times. They are a beautiful reminder of the heritage of quilting, and each time I make a traditional block, such as this star, it reminds me of how I've stepped into the ritual of quilting, as countless other makers have done before me. There is so much beauty in the history of quilting and it gives me tremendous pleasure to continue the practice.

SIZE	IMPERIAL	METRIC
Baby	44 x 44in	112 x 112cm

This pattern can easily be scaled up or down to suit your needs. To learn more about scaling, please see Scaling Patterns on page 24.

SCALING SUGGESTIONS
▶ *Queen*: Scale by 200 per cent to make a quilt that finishes at 88 x 88in or 224 x 224cm
▶ *Mini*: Scale by 50 per cent to make a quilt that finishes at 22 x 22in or 56 x 56cm

MATERIALS
The default instructions are written for standard fabric with a width of 42in or 107cm. Variations for wide fabric with a width of 54in or 137cm are indicated in the table opposite and given in parentheses in the cutting instructions: Standard (Wide).

▶ Dark Fabric: Essex Yarn-Dyed Lingerie
▶ Light Fabric: Essex Ivory wide
▶ Backing: Essex Natural wide
▶ Binding: Essex Ivory wide
▶ Batting: Quilters Dream Wool

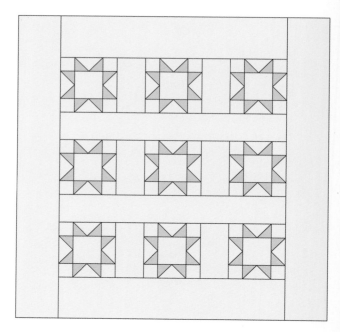

ASSEMBLY DIAGRAM

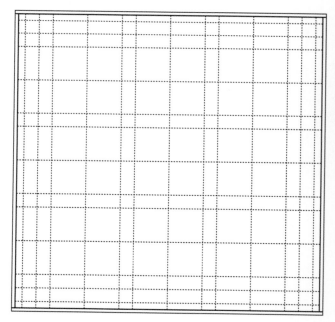

QUILTING GUIDE

BABY

Fabric	Imperial		Metric	
	Standard (42in)	Wide (54in)	Standard (107cm)	Wide (137cm)
Dark	½yd	⅜yd	50cm	35cm
Light	2⅜yd	1⅔yd	2.2m	1.55m
Backing	3yd	1½yd	2.75m	1.4m
Batting	46 x 46in	46 x 46in	117 x 117cm	117 x 117cm
Binding	½yd	⅜yd	50cm	35cm

CUTTING INSTRUCTIONS

From the Dark Fabric, cut:
▶ 5 (4) strips 2½in x WOF. Subcut:
  ▶ 72 squares 2½ x 2½in

From the Light Fabric, cut:
▶ 6 (4) strips 6½in x WOF. Subcut:
  ▶ 4 strips 6½ x 22½in
  (2 strips 6½ x 44½in)
  ▶ 2 (2) strips 6½ x 32½in
▶ 4 (3) strips 4½in x WOF. Subcut:
  ▶ 2 strips 4½ x 32½in
  ▶ 6 rectangles 4½ x 8½in
  ▶ 9 squares 4½ x 4½in
▶ 7 (5) strips 2½in x WOF. Subcut:
  ▶ 36 rectangles 2½ x 4½in
  ▶ 36 squares 2½ x 2½in

From the Backing Fabric, cut:
▶ Standard: 2 pieces 54in x WOF
▶ Wide: 1 piece 54in x WOF

From the Batting, cut:
▶ 1 piece 46 x 46in (117 x 117cm)

From the Binding Fabric, cut:
▶ 5 (4) 2½in x WOF strips

SEWING INSTRUCTIONS

MAKE THE FLYING-GEESE UNITS

1. On the wrong side of the dark 2½ x 2½in squares, mark a diagonal line from corner to corner.

2. Place a dark 2½ x 2½in square on top of a light 2½ x 4½in rectangle, with right sides together so the line is facing up as shown (Diagram 1).

Diagram 1

3. Sew along the marked line. Then trim off the excess, cutting ¼in away from the seam as shown (Diagram 2).

Diagram 2

4. Using an iron, press the seam open (Diagram 3).

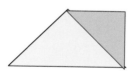

Diagram 3

5. Place a second dark 2½ x 2½in square on the other side of the flying-geese unit as shown (Diagram 4). Sew along the marked line and trim off the excess, cutting ¼in away from the seam (Diagram 5).

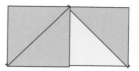 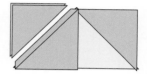

Diagram 4   Diagram 5

6. Press the seam open, then finish the unit by trimming it to 2½ x 4½in, making sure you leave ¼in above the point (Diagram 6).

Diagram 6

7. Repeat Steps 2–6 until you have made 36 flying-geese units.

MAKE THE STAR BLOCKS

8. Using two flying-geese units and one light 4½ x 4½in square, begin to construct the centre of the first star block. Sew a flying-geese unit to either side of one light 4½ x 4½in square as shown (Diagram 7). Press the seams open and set aside. Repeat to make nine star-block centre units.

Diagram 7

9. Using one flying-geese unit and two light 2½ x 2½in squares, begin to construct the outer edges of the star block. Sew one light 2½ x 2½in square to either side of a flying-geese unit as shown (Diagram 8). Press the seams open and set aside. Repeat to make 18 outer-edge units.

Diagram 8

10. Make up the first star block, using one star-block centre unit and two outer-edge units. Sew one outer-edge unit to the top of the centre unit and one outer-edge unit to the bottom as shown (Diagram 9). Press the seams open to finish the star block. Repeat to make a total of nine star blocks.

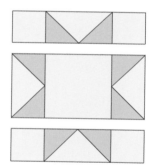

Diagram 9

TIP
Match the seams together carefully and pin in place before sewing to keep the corners neat and tidy.

ASSEMBLE THE QUILT TOP

11. Using three star blocks and two light 4½ x 8½in rectangles in between them, assemble a row as shown (Diagram 10). Press the seams open and repeat to form three rows in total.

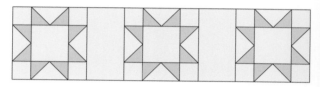

Diagram 10

12. Sew the rows together, with the two light 4½ x 32½in strips in between, as shown (Diagram 11). Press the seams open.

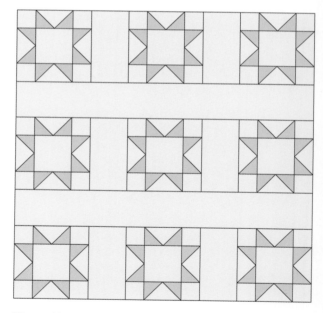

Diagram 11

13. Attach the top and bottom borders by sewing one 6½ x 32½in strip to the top of the quilt top and the other to the bottom as shown (Diagram 12). Press the seams open.

Diagram 12

14. If you are using standard-width fabric, sew two light 6½ x 22½in strips together, end to end, to form a strip of 6½ x 44½in. Repeat to make a second strip of 6½ x 44½in. If you are using wide fabric, skip this step.

15. Attach the side borders by sewing the 6½ x 44½in strips to the left and right sides of the quilt (Diagram 13). Press the seams open to finish.

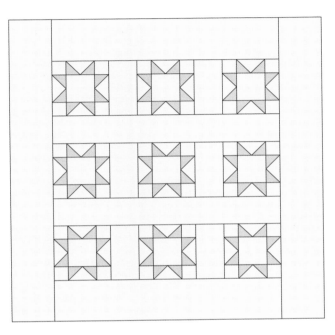

Diagram 13

ASSEMBLING THE QUILT
Refer to pages 36–51 for assembling, quilting and binding your quilt. Turn to page 170 for the assembly diagram and quilting guide.

QUILTING SUGGESTIONS
To finish your quilt like the one pictured, mark your quilting lines as follows:

▶ Through the horizontal and vertical centres of each star.

▶ 1in (2.5cm) to the left and right of each star block.

▶ 1in (2.5cm) above and below each star block.

▶ In 2in (5cm) increments from each marked line in the outer borders.

RALLY

Everyone needs a good jacket, and I really enjoy giving a new-to-me garment a "quilty" spin. The Rally design offers a starting point to create a panel that you can customize for your own jacket and style. I love the hourglass shape created by this pattern, and how the quilting adds an extra-chic touch. This design reminds me of going places with friends, bringing that extra layer "just in case", and the energy that comes with not knowing where the day (or night) might take you.

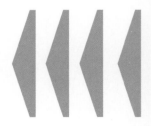

SIZE	IMPERIAL	METRIC
Jacket Panel*	11 x 17in	28 x 43cm

Finished size may vary depending on your jacket size

MATERIALS

For this project, you'll need a jacket with a back panel that you can modify, which should measure at least 6 x 16in (15 x 41cm). Find a jacket in a colour and style that speak to you – and, most importantly, make sure it fits well. No batting, backing or binding fabric is required for this project because the pieced panel is stitched onto the back panel of the jacket using appliqué.

The default instructions are written for standard width of fabric with a width of 42in or 107cm. Due to the small size of this project, there is no difference in the instructions or materials needed if using wide fabric. Variations for wide fabric with a width of 54in or 137cm are indicated in the table opposite and given in parentheses in the cutting instructions: Standard (Wide).

▶ Dark Fabric: Brussels Washer Yarn-Dyed Redrock
▶ Light Fabric: Essex Natural wide

ASSEMBLY DIAGRAM

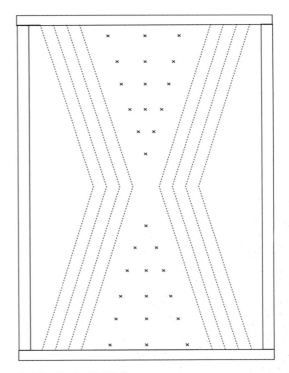

QUILTING GUIDE

JACKET PANEL

Fabric	Imperial Standard (42in) or Wide (54in)	Metric Standard (107cm) or Wide (137cm)
Dark	¼yd	25cm
Light	¼yd	25cm

CUTTING INSTRUCTIONS

You will need to adjust the pattern to fit your specific jacket.

The top and bottom borders may need to be cut wider than 1in, and you may need to cut more or fewer strips to create a panel that works for your jacket. Please read through all the instructions before beginning so you can plan accordingly.

From the Dark Fabric, cut:
▶ 1 strip 4in x WOF. Subcut:
  ▶ 2 rectangles 4 x 17in
▶ 2 strips* 1in x WOF. Subcut:
  ▶ 4 strips 1 x 16½in (side strips)

From the Light Fabric, cut:
▶ 1 strip 5½in x WOF. Subcut:
  ▶ 2 rectangles 5½ x 9in
▶ 3 strips* 1in x WOF. Subcut:
  ▶ 6 strips 1 x 16½in (side strips)
  ▶ 2 strips 1 x 11½in (top and bottom borders)

SEWING INSTRUCTIONS

PREPARE THE JACKET TEMPLATE

1. Lay out your jacket as flat as possible with the back panel facing up. Lay a piece of tracing paper or light scrap fabric over the top and trace the shape of the back panel just inside the seams to make a template. Mark a ¼in (6mm) seam allowance around the entire template and cut out along the seam allowance line. Measure the approximate size of your panel at its widest points and write down the dimensions – the example is approximately 11 x 17in (28 x 43cm). Set the jacket template aside until Step 10.

2. You will need to alter the quilt pattern to fit your jacket. The centre portion (Diagram 1) finishes at 6 x 16in (15 x 41cm). You can adjust the height by increasing or decreasing the depth of the top and bottom borders, and you can adjust the width by altering the number of 1in strips you use.

Diagram 1

PREPARE THE PIECING TEMPLATES

3. Download and print out the piecing templates from riane-elise.com/quilting-by-hand.

4. Fold one of the dark 4 x 17in rectangles in half lengthways and, using an iron, press the fold flat. Place the A template on the folded 4 x 8½in rectangle, lining up the folded edge with the edge indicated on the template. Trace the shape and cut it out. Repeat to make a second A piece.

5. Place the B template on the light 5½ x 9in rectangle. Trace the shape and cut it out. Repeat to make a second B piece.

ASSEMBLE THE PANEL

6. Place a light B triangle on top of a dark A piece, with right sides together (Diagram 2). Line up the blunt edge of the light triangle flush with the edge of the dark piece and sew in place using a standard ¼in seam. Press the seam open and set aside. Repeat to make another A/B piece in the same manner.

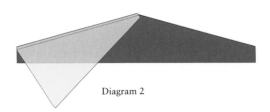

Diagram 2

7. Sew the two A/B pieces you made in Step 6 together as shown (Diagram 3). Press the seam open.

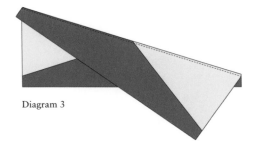

Diagram 3

8. Sew alternating light and dark 1in strips to the left and right sides of the centre piece as shown (Diagram 4). In this example three light and two dark strips were added on each side, but you may need to use more or fewer 1in strips to fit your jacket panel. Press all the seams open as you sew. Continue adding alternating strips until your panel is at least ½in wider than the jacket template that you created in Step 1.

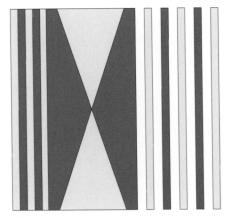

Diagram 4

9. You may need to adjust the depth of the top and bottom borders to fully cover your jacket panel. Cut your top and bottom borders so your finished panel will be at least ½in longer than the jacket template that you created in Step 1. Sew the top and bottom borders to your centre piece and press open (Diagram 5).

Diagram 5

TRIM TO SIZE

10. Once the panel is sewn together, trim it to the size needed for your jacket. Lay the jacket template from Step 1 on top of the right side of the panel you've created, making sure the template is centred (see image 1). Cut along the marked line you just created (see image 2).

ATTACH THE PANEL

11. The panel is attached to the back of the jacket using appliqué. Centre the panel over the back of your jacket and pin it in place using safety pins or straight pins. Carefully fold the raw edges under by ¼in so they are hidden and the edges of the panel are flush with the jacket seams. Use a whipstitch or appliqué stitch (refer to appliqué section on page 52) ties to secure the panel to the jacket, working your way evenly around the edges.

QUILTING SUGGESTIONS

To finish your jacket panel like the one pictured, mark your quilting lines as follows:

▶ Mark lines parallel to the pieced seams, beginning 1in (2.5cm) to the left and right of the diagonal seams. Continue marking parallel lines at 1in (5cm) intervals. Mark small dots in the center triangles at staggered intervals for criss-cross ties.

TIP

It's important to include the ¼in around the template when tracing so you can turn the edges under during appliqué. This ensures that the panel finishes flush with the seams of your jacket.

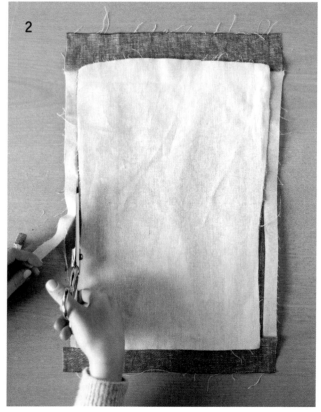

GREETING

Adding a feeling of warmth and comfort to any room, cushions are the perfect home accessory. This pair of Greeting cushions is a fun project for when you want to make something new and unique for your home. The curves are attached to the cushion top with appliqué, another form of handwork in which one piece of fabric is sewn on top of another. This pattern is perfect for a playful hand-quilting finish, such as tying, which will add another layer of texture as well as a touch of whimsy.

SIZE Cushions 1 & 2
IMPERIAL 18 x 18in (fits 18 x 18in cushion)
METRIC 46 x 46cm (fits 45 x 45cm cushion)

MATERIALS

▶ Dark Fabric: Brussels Washer O.D.
  Green , Essex Putty
▶ Light Fabric: Essex Ivory wide
▶ Backing: Essex Ivory wide
▶ Envelope Closures: Brussels Washer O.D.
  Green, Essex Putty
▶ Batting: Quilters Dream Wool

CUSHION 1

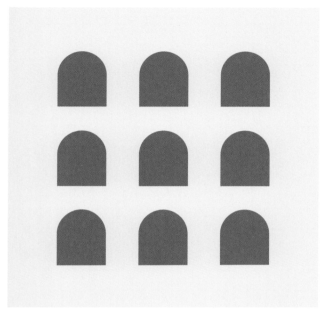

CUSHION 1 ASSEMBLY DIAGRAM

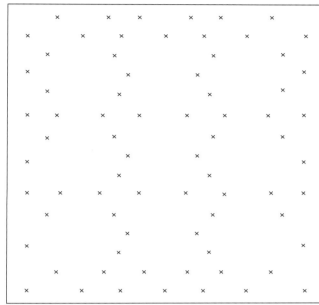

CUSHION 1 QUILTING GUIDE

Fabric	Imperial Standard (42in) or Wide (54in)	Metric Standard (107cm) or Wide (137cm)
Dark	⅛yd	15cm
Light	⅝yd	60cm
Backing	20 x 20in	55 x 55cm
Batting	19½ x 19½in	50 x 50cm
Envelope closures	½yd	50cm

CUTTING INSTRUCTIONS

From the Dark Fabric, cut:
▶ 1 strip 3¼in x WOF. Subcut:
  ▶ 9 rectangles 3¼ x 3¾in

From the Light Fabric, cut:
▶ 1 square 19 x 19in (cushion top)

From the Backing Fabric, cut:
▶ 1 square 20 x 20in

From the Batting, cut:
▶ 1 piece 19½ x 19½in (50 x 50cm)

From the Envelope Closure Fabric, cut:
▶ 2 rectangles 14½ x 18½in

CUSHION 2

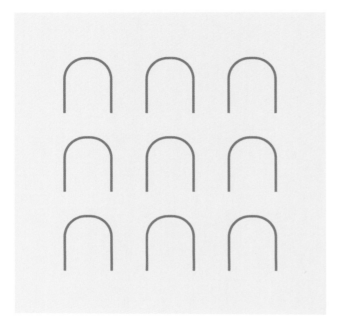

CUSHION 2 ASSEMBLY DIAGRAM

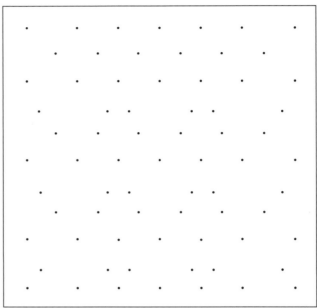

CUSHION 2 QUILTING GUIDE

Fabric	Imperial Standard (42in) or Wide (54in)	Metric Standard (107cm) or Wide (137cm)
Dark	½yd	50cm
Light	⅝yd	60cm
Backing	20 x 20in	55 x 55cm
Batting	19½ x 19½in	50 x 50cm
Envelope closures	½yd	50cm

CUTTING INSTRUCTIONS

From the Dark Fabric, cut:
▶ 1 square 13 x 13in

From the Light Fabric, cut:
▶ 1 square 19 x 19in (cushion top)

From the Backing Fabric, cut:
▶ 1 square 20 x 20in

From the Batting, cut:
▶ 1 piece 19½ x 19½in (50 x 50cm)

From the Envelope Closure Fabric, cut:
▶ 2 rectangles 14½ x 18½in

SEWING INSTRUCTIONS

PREPARE THE TEMPLATES AND PIECES

1. Print out the templates from riane-elise.com/quilting-by-hand and cut them out.

CUSHION 1

2. Place the A template on top of each of the dark 3¼ x 3¾in rectangles and trace the shape. Cut out the curved fabric pieces.

CUSHION 2

3. Using the 45-degree line on your quilting ruler, mark and then cut the dark 13 x 13in square along the diagonal in 1in strips as shown (Diagram 1). You do not need to cut the whole square – begin cutting where the strips will be at least 9in long, and cut at least nine strips. Trim the nine strips so they are all 9in long.

Diagram 1

4. For each strip, turn one long edge under by about a third and press with an iron (Diagram 2).

Diagram 2

MARK THE CUSHION TOPS

FOR CUSHIONS 1 AND 2

5. Using a hera marker or light marking tool, mark a line 3in from both sides and 2¾in from the top and bottom edges as shown (Diagram 3).

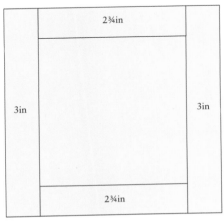

Diagram 3

6. Place the B template inside the marked lines, as shown, and trace lightly around it in each of the four corners with an erasable marking tool (Diagram 4).

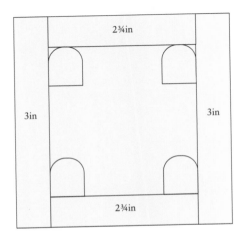

Diagram 4

7. Using your hera marker or light marking tool once again, mark a line 2in to the right of the left-hand shapes, and 2in to the left of the right-hand shapes. Mark another line 1½in below the bottom of the top shapes and 1½in above the tops of the bottom shapes (Diagram 5).

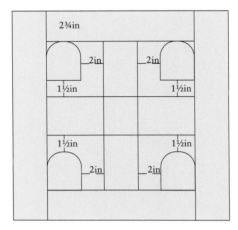

Diagram 5

8. Place the B template inside the marked lines, as shown, and trace lightly around it in each of the five positions with an erasable marking tool (Diagram 6).

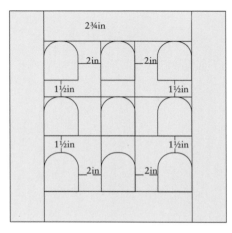

Diagram 6

APPLIQUÉ THE CUSHION TOP

Refer to the appliqué techniques on page 52 for instructions on how to attach the feature fabric to the cushion top fabric.

CUSHION 1

9. Centre one of the dark curved pieces over one of the curved outlines you marked on the cushion top. Baste in place.

10. Tuck the edges of the dark piece under about ⅛–¼in (3–6mm), and use a blind stitch or whipstitch (see page 190) tow them to the cushion top. Continue tucking the raw edges under and sewing around the curve until the dark piece is fully affixed to the cushion top (Diagram 7).

Diagram 7

11. Repeat Steps 9–10 to appliqué all the dark curved pieces to the cushion top. Once complete, erase any remaining marks to finish the cushion top.

CUSHION 2

12. Align the folded edge of one of the nine dark fabric strips to one of the curves you marked on the cushion top, with the wrong side of the strip to the right side of the cushion top (Diagram 8). Baste in place.

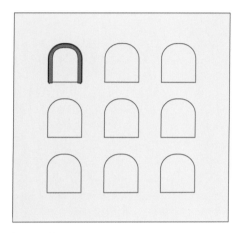

Diagram 8

13. Use a blind stitch or whipstitch to appliqué the folded edge to the marked line. Start at one end and sew around the curve.

14. Once you've sewn around the outer curve, trim the ends of the strip on that side if needed and tuck them under by about ¼in (6mm). Appliqué the ends of the strip and then turn your work to sew the inner curve. Fold the raw edge under and tuck it with your needle as you stitch to take up the excess fabric. The width of the finished strip should be about ½in.

15. When you reach the final edge of the strip, turn the raw edges under by about ¼in. Appliqué in place to finish the strip.

16. Repeat Steps 12–15 to appliqué the remaining eight strips on the corresponding curves. Once complete, erase any remaining marks to finish the cushion top.

FINISHING THE CUSHIONS
QUILT THE CUSHION TOPS

17. Make your quilt sandwich by layering the backing, batting and cushion top, and pinning them in place (see page 39). Quilt as desired. Trim the square to 19 x 19in.

QUILTING SUGGESTIONS

To finish your cushions like the ones pictured, mark your tying lines as follows:

▶ Mark small dots 1-2in (2.5–5cm) apart throughout the cushion top to indicate where ties should go.

SEW THE ENVELOPE CLOSURES

Refer to the finishing cushions section on page 53 for instructions on how to create envelope closures for your cushions.

GLOSSARY

APPLIQUÉ To sew one piece of fabric to the top of another piece of fabric.

BACKING The bottom or back layer of a quilt.

BACKSTITCH To sew backwards by one or several stitches, either by hand or machine. Often used to secure or stabilize a seam.

BASTING To temporarily hold all the layers of a quilt together while quilting. Often done using safety pins or basting stitches. Also called tracking.

BATTING The lofty inner layer of a quilt, often made from wool or cotton. Also called wadding.

BINDING To finish a quilt by enclosing its raw edges with fabric after quilting. Often the last step of the quilting process.

BLIND STITCH A useful stitch for appliqué and binding. To make a blind stitch, start by tying a knot in one end of your thread. Bring the needle and thread up through the layers you are sewing, catching the binding or appliqué fabric. Insert the needle through the background or backing fabric close to the prior insertion point, and bring the needle up through the binding or appliqué fabric again about 1/8–1/4in (3–6mm) away from the prior stitch. Repeat to continue the stitch.

FRENCH KNOT An embroidery stitch made by wrapping thread around the needle. This stitch can be used for hand tying quilts.

INVISIBLE STITCH A type of hand stitch used for binding and appliqué, which produces small, almost invisible stitches.

MARKING Using a marking tool to draw a stitching line on fabric, often used to mark hand piecing or quilting lines.

MARKING TOOL A pen, pencil, marker or hera marker used for marking quilting or stitching lines. Often erasable or temporary.

PATCHWORK A name for a section of fabric or quilt top that has been constructed by sewing multiple pieces of fabric together.

PIECING The practice of sewing individual fabric pieces together to create patchwork.

PINS Straight pins are used to hold fabric together during the piecing or patchwork process. Safety pins are used to baste the layers together for quilting.

PRESSING Using a hot iron to smooth out seams or fabric.

QUILT SANDWICH The three layers of a quilt – backing, batting or wadding and the quilt top.

QUILTING To stitch all layers of a quilt together with thread.

QUILTING LINES Marked lines on a quilt top that indicate where one should place quilting stitches.

QUILTING RULER Often featuring a clear plastic face and lines at 1/8in intervals. A quilting ruler is a great tool for cutting fabric pieces and for marking piecing and quilting lines.

SASHIKO A style of Japanese visible stitching. While not specifically made in the Japanese sashiko style, quilts in this book were made using sashiko needles and thread.

SEAM ALLOWANCE The excess fabric left after sewing two pieces of fabric together. In quilting, the standard seam allowance is 1/4in.

SQUARE UP To trim the quilt to its finished size after quilting. This is one of the last steps, right before binding.

STITCH LENGTH The length of a stitch on the top and bottom (can refer to machine-made or handmade stitches).

TOPSTITCH To sew a line of stitching over the top of your fabric, usually with a machine. Most commonly used for finishing seams and hems.

TEMPLATES Shapes traced onto fabric and cut out to form patchwork pieces that are difficult to cut with a standard quilting ruler.

TYING To finish a quilt with small stitches that are tied using a square knot.

WADDING See batting.

WALKING FOOT A sewing-machine attachment that feeds fabric more evenly through a sewing machine. It is especially helpful for binding or sewing over several layers of fabric, or over a quilt sandwich.

WHIPSTITCH A useful stitch for appliqué and binding. To make a whipstitch, start by tying a knot in one end of your thread. Bring the needle and thread up through the layers you are sewing, catching the binding or appliqué fabric. Insert the needle through the background or backing fabric about 1/8–1/4in (3–6mm) away from the prior stitch. Bring the needle up again about 1/8–1/4in (3–6mm) away from the prior stitch. Repeat to continue the stitch.

RESOURCES

The fabric used in this book was generously supplied by Robert Kaufman Fabrics, and includes selections of Essex Linen, Essex Yarn-Dyed Linen and Brussels Washer Linen Blend. The batting is Dream Wool by Quilters Dream. The hand-quilting thread is sashiko thread by Upcycle Stitches, including commercially manufactured threads by Coron Thread Company and naturally hand-dyed threads by Keiko Futatsuya of Sashi.Co.

FABRICS USED IN THIS BOOK
▶ Robert Kaufman Essex Ivory wide (E024-1181)
▶ Robert Kaufman Essex Natural wide (E024-1242)
▶ Robert Kaufman Essex Yarn-Dyed Lingerie (E064-843)
▶ Robert Kaufman Essex Peach (E014-1281)
▶ Robert Kaufman Essex Leather (E014-178)
▶ Robert Kaufman Essex Ochre (E064-1704)
▶ Robert Kaufman Essex Putty (E014-1303)
▶ Robert Kaufman Brussels Washer Yarn-Dyed Redrock (B142-553)
▶ Robert Kaufman Brussels Washer O.D. Green (B031-1256)

BATTING
▶ Quilters Dream Wool by Quilters Dream

THREAD
▶ Kakishibu Sashiko Thread by Keiko Futatsuya of Sashi.Co (#K3, Kakishibu Brown/Beige)
▶ Natural Dye Sashiko Thread by Keiko Futatsuya of Sashi.Co (#013m, Western Madder)
▶ Natural Dye Sashiko Thread by Keiko Futatsuya of Sashi.Co (#004, Tangala)
▶ Coron Thread Company Original White (#10), obtained in partnership with UpCycle Stitches
▶ Wonderfil Konfetti 50-weight Egyptian Cotton, various colours
▶ Aurifil 50-weight cotton thread, various colours

NEEDLES
▶ Tulip Sashiko Needles Assorted Long Tulip Needles (#THN-030E)
▶ John James Sharps, size 3/9 (#JJ11039)

Special thanks to the team at Robert Kaufman Fabrics for helping to make the quilts in this book come to life with their beautiful fabric.

upcyclestitches.com
robertkaufman.com
wonderfil.ca
aurifil.com
en.tulip-japan.co.jp
jjneedles.com

Shop the supplies from this book at materialgoods.us.

UK SUPPLIERS
▶ raystitch.co.uk
▶ eternalmaker.com
▶ thesewingstudio.co.uk
▶ merchantandmills.com

AUSTRALIAN SUPPLIERS
▶ sewmondo.com.au
▶ scribblygumquiltco.com
▶ thenextstitch.com.au
▶ myfabricology.com.au

ACKNOWLEDGEMENTS

This book would not be possible without the help and support of some incredible people. I owe them all my gratitude (and a glass of wine the next time we meet).

Thank you to my amazing family for instilling in me a love of making. Thank you, Mom, for making that first quilt for me, for providing creative outlets from before I can remember and for teaching me the art of mental toughness. Thank you, Dad, for the endless maths lessons and for promising me that one day they would come in handy (I hate that you were right). Thank you to my grandmothers – Gerry, who taught me how to quilt, and Betty, who always has one of my quilts on the bed, or my latest work on the coffee table. And thank you to all the others who have supported me in so many ways on my journey.

Thank you to my sister, Erin, for being my go-to creative advisor and my first critic and consultant about all things design. You keep me inspired and grounded, and I'm still learning from you what it means to be content in work and in life.

To my quilting friends, Molly and Amanda, thank you for being some of the first to see the designs and cheering me on throughout the process, especially during the hard times. Thank you to Jessie, Erin and Carol, for always being there for me, no matter what. Thank you to Yvonne for once again working your magic to make these patterns airtight. You're the absolute best. And thank you to Deb, my quilting guide, my forever cheerleader, and one of my best friends and mentors for setting my feet so firmly and confidently on this path.

Thank you to Harriet for being the absolute best editor I could ask for, and for taking a chance on me. Your thoughtful guidance and considered edits have made this book better than I ever could have imagined. Thank you for steering this ship with such grace, even through a global pandemic. Thank you to Gemma for your amazing design and for guiding this book into its gorgeous final form. Thank you to Rebecca Stumpf and Molly O'Connell for bringing the quilts to life with such beauty and polish. Thank you to Macy and Laura for letting us into your homes, and thank you to Reanne Alise for lending your beauty and grace to this project. Thanks also to my amazing family, Matthew, Ellie, and Mary, for bringing your joyful, smiling faces to our shoot. And lastly, thank you to Zia and the whole Quadrille team for helping with the finishing touches.

Thank you to everyone who has cheered me along in this journey in some way, especially on social media. You are a constant source of inspiration, love and joy in my life, and your support has spurred me onwards in ways that you can never know.

Thanks to Dallas, for loving me unconditionally and reminding me to take breaks, stretch my legs, enjoy the fresh air and smell the flowers.

And finally, thank you (now and forever) to my husband, Kevin. Thanks for letting me cover the house in thread, for helping me hunt for the pins I drop and for holding up quilts for me to inspect; and thanks for believing in me every step of the way, whatever life throws at us. I promise I will make a quilt for our bed someday.

ABOUT THE AUTHOR

Riane Menardi Morrison, who quilts by the name
of Riane Elise, is a modern quilter and textile artist
living and working near Denver, Colorado. She crafts
heirloom-quality quilts that are primarily made and
quilted by hand, using the traditions taught to her by
her grandmother. She believes deeply in quilting as
a beautiful and functional practice that connects us
with past generations, providing a link between a rich
textile heritage and modern design and handcraft. She
considers quilting part of her inheritance, and loves to
introduce new quilters to this rich sewing tradition.

You can connect with Riane at riane-elise.com or on
Instagram @riane.elise.